CRASHAW
AND THE
BAROQUE

CRASHAW
AND THE
BAROQUE

by
MARC F. BERTONASCO

THE UNIVERSITY OF ALABAMA PRESS
University, Alabama

In Memory of
HELEN C. WHITE

Copyright © 1971 by
The University of Alabama Press
ISBN 0-8173-7308-X
Library of Congress Catalog Card Number 70-148692
Manufactured in the United States of America

PREFACE

Dr. Bertonasco's book is both learned and intuitive, original and honest in itself, and, as well, richly serviceable to a genuine need—even though the subject is a seventeenth-century English poet and the time some fifty-five years after the beginning of a great seventeenth-century revival. Seventeenth-century English poetry has been fashionable in the twentieth, but not that of Richard Crashaw, who is less read today than most of his comparable contemporaries— read with less understanding, and liked or disliked for the wrong reasons. Of course there are and should be more critical works on Jonson, Donne, and Milton, whose volume, range, and creative power are greater, and on Marvell, whose work reflects the complexities of a transitional era. But Crashaw has been neglected as compared with George Herbert and in contrast to both Herbert and Vaughan has fared badly at the hands of the critics.

At about the time he wrote *The Hound of Heaven*, Francis Thompson was finding Crashaw to be only a little less than Shelley and Shelley to be only a little less than Shakespeare. "To most people," Thompson wrote, "the Metaphysical School means Donne, whereas it ought to mean Crashaw. We judge the direction of a development by its highest form, though that form may have been produced but once and produced imperfectly. Now the highest product of the Metaphysical School was Crashaw, and Crashaw was a Shelley manqué . . . The Metaphysical School, like Shelley, loved imagery for its own sake."

Thompson's last sentence touches the heart of the Crashaw problem, as Dr. Bertonasco has made clear. No one familiar with Renaissance iconography in all its many and various traditional crystallizations of ideas—especially emblem literature—could credit the baroque or metaphysical poets with "imagery for its own sake." If Thompson overrated Crashaw through lack of appreciation, the prevailing trend of twentieth-century criticism has been to underrate him because of the same lack of understanding of the same stylistic traits. What for Thompson was "rapturous ethereality" for Robert M. Adams was "grotesque." (It is true, of course, that Thompson may have had "The Flaming Heart" chiefly in mind, and Adams "The Weeper.") Many later critics have, like Thompson, ignored the age and that special culture of which Crashaw's poetry is a representative, sometimes a transcendent, expression. As our author says, "No poet has suffered more than Crashaw from a failure on the part of critics to make the necessary historical orientation."

That orientation and its light are the achievement of this book, which treats Crashaw's distinctive style as his rather special response to influences of his time—the rich contemporary iconography and the practice of Salesian (as opposed to Ignation) meditation. These influences determined *what he did* with emblematic imagery and *how* he handled "the emblematic mode of expression," which was not always a borrowing of emblematic commonplaces. Dr. Bertonasco suggests that the Crashavian paradox of icons that are totally sensuous but also "curiously unreal" can be understood in terms of the degree and stage of meditation which they realize. He makes it very clear why this emblematic imagery differs from Donne's in such sententious poems as "A Valediction Forbidding Mourning" and "A Lecture Upon the Shadow." In Donne's poems, borrowings from the emblem books are distilled into something other than emblems, but these are not divine emblems and are not found in the divine poems. Crashaw's remain in "the emblematic mode." The graphicness of that mode, which has given offense to some modern readers of Crashaw, Dr. Bertonasco describes as common to Crashaw and certain minor but popular emblematic poets such as Quarles, who lacked Crashaw's power and creativeness but were widely read in their own time, and he suggests that Crashaw's affiliations are with a more ordinary school than that of the great metaphysical poets.

Though this could be an argument for Crashaw's inferiority to them after all, such an impression is dispelled by Dr. Bertonasco's studies of individual poems—of some of "The Divine Epigrams," and most particularly by his sensitive explication of "The Weeper," which has been lamentably misunderstood. Through these studies he succeeds in making Crashaw more knowable to twentieth-century readers and the limitations of his knowability more understandable. What emerges is poetry that is pure and true. Though this book is, as its author says, historically oriented, he has not forgotten to be a critic—nor that his subject is a poet.

Linda Van Norden

Contents

CRASHAW
AND THE
BAROQUE

INTRODUCTION

Lip-smacking cherubs and bleeding hearts, sparkling pearls
and delicious deaths—these are among the images which the
name of Richard Crashaw is sure to evoke in the minds of
most readers. Although "cloyingly sweet and exotic," Crashaw
is still granted a few days' study in seventeenth-century
courses, for, it is said, his tawdry rhetoric and Baroque grotesqueness occasionally give way to inspired rhapsodical
flights of undeniable beauty. A fairly accurate appreciation
of Crashaw's art is to be found in the pioneer studies of Helen
White, Ruth Wallerstein, and Austin Warren; but at least
twelve fairly recent studies—including the important books
of Alvarez, Bennett, de Mourgues, and Watkin—prove that
the views of these scholars are neither universally accepted
nor nearly so widely understood as they might be. Presumably, these publications (ignoring or attacking the studies
of White, Wallerstein, and Warren) have made some impact,
for most references to Crashaw, in anthologies and general
studies, are mildly pejorative or condescending. And the
Warnke-Witherspoon text, now the most widely used one
in seventeenth-century courses, includes, in its short list

of studies recommended to the undergraduate, the *Metaphysical, Baroque and Precieux Poetry*, by Odette de Mourgues, who sees Crashaw's esthetic as essentially a "pandering to the basest emotions in the name of religion," and who finds in his religious lyrics little but a "distorted" view of life and numerous perversions. My own experience with colleagues and students further convinces me that the most common verdict is still that of T. S. Eliot, who, after pointing to the intellectual element in Crashaw, labeled it "perverse."

The purpose of this book is to readjust the popular image of Crashaw, to suggest several new lines of approach to his religious lyrics, and to demonstrate that this major poet exercises a far firmer control over his materials than critics have generally recognized. The first chapter has two purposes: to counter those critical opinions which ignore or attack the studies of White, Wallerstein, and Warren, and to present, for the general student, a method of explicating a Crashaw lyric. The knowledgeable scholar may at times question the necessity to go to such lengths in "translating" the imagery, but recent studies indicate that such detailed treatment would be useful, at least for the general student. Perhaps of greater interest to the scholar, in this chapter, is the tracing of Crashaw's key images to seventeenth-century emblem books to silence that critical school which denies the emblematic nature of Crashaw's imagery.

To study Crashaw's imagery in a historical vacuum yields unsatisfactory results. No poet has suffered more than Crashaw from a failure on the part of critics to make the necessary historical orientation. Scholarly readers ignore the emblem tradition, so popular in seventeenth-century England, and fail to perceive that those elements labeled (even by Austin Warren) as "continental" or "Catholic" were not the exclusive property of Counter-Reformation countries, but pervaded the air in England. Consequently, these received critics regard Crashaw as a *rara avis* which they cannot neatly place in the mainstream of English literature. Following Praz, they carelessly label "Marinistic" whatever in Crashaw seems exotic to them. Anthologies have followed suit. The second chapter demonstrates that, as one leaves the aristocratic literary tradition of seventeenth-century England, he finds with amazing frequency open manifestations of the more sensuous, grotesque, energetic elements of the Baroque esthetic. Viewed in this new historical perspective, Crashaw no longer appears exotic. Surprisingly, he shares with a certain segment of contemporary English Puritans several traits which scholars have far too hastily labeled Roman Catholic. In the religious life of the seventeenth century there are no water-tight compartments: thus, not surprisingly, a major influence on the spiritual formation of Crashaw was St. Francis de Sales, Bishop of Geneva. The Salesian—not the Ignatian—method of meditation profoundly affected Crashaw's poetic method, and especially his structure. This study will try to demonstrate not only *that* but also *how* Salesian meditation is exemplified in the tone, mood, and disposition of images in Crashaw's major poems.

The third chapter presents a detailed analysis of a Baroque verse meditation—"The Weeper"—to tie neatly together, and to illustrate in action, the major points developed in the first two chapters; and to present a fresh interpretation and appreciation of the most notorious poem of the English Renaissance. The appendix offers a historical survey and assessment of Crashaw scholarship during the twentieth century, and a complete bibliography.

CRASHAW
AND THE
EMBLEM

Nothing ties Crashaw more securely to the early seventeenth century than his use of the emblem. Indeed, the mental exertion that this literary device demands cannot be disassociated from the Baroque religious poet, who is concerned to enlist the aid of the senses to grasp a spiritual truth and thus turns so frequently to the emblem, not primarily for its value as picture or sensation but to express the thought which this symbol embodies. The emblem, which is at the base of Crashaw's poems, can be either contracted or greatly extended. Crashaw makes use of both types. And it is apparent that the emblem lends itself to several forms of thought; not surprisingly, for this age which saw in art a two-fold function, to teach and to delight, developed the emblem chiefly as a didactic tool. It can, for example, be an instrument of explication or psychological analysis, as it was for Donne. Or it can be an instrument of contemplation, as it almost always was for Crashaw.

Nor should it be thought that such ingenuity as the emblem obviously requires is in any sense incompatible with the expresson of contemplative thought. It is difficult perhaps for the modern reader to believe that such a highly rhetorical method of writing as the Baroque represents is compatible with seriousness of *any* kind, but seventeenth-century man resorted to wit in those very critical circumstances of life which usually elicit simple expressions today even from the most sophisticated of men. Donne, on the day when all hopes of happiness seemed to forsake him, found nothing better than a witticism: "John Donne, Anne Donne, Undone." And Mr. Praz quotes Pierfrancesco Minozzi (*Sfogamenti d'ingegno,* Venice, 1641) who, although he cannot approve of conceits in profane stories, praises them in devotional works, especially in the lives of the saints.[1] This point may seem belabored, but it is essential that a reader of Baroque poetry grant from the start that the poet is sincere and that his purpose may be serious.

Indeed, so adaptable is the emblem to even the most serious of purposes that Crashaw, writing in great earnestness to persuade the Countess of Denbigh to embrace the Roman Catholic Church, uses this very device:

> What fatall, yet fantastick bands
> Keep the free Heart from it's own hands!
> So when the year takes cold, we see
> Poor waters their owne prisoners be.
> Fetter'd and lockt up fast they ly
> In a sad selfe-captivity.
> > (Martin's 2nd rev. ed. Oxford, 1957)

"How concrete this figure renders a thought very difficult to express directly," writes George Williamson.[2]

But as Mr. Williamson goes on to discuss the conceits in the meditative lyrics, he strikes progressively less enthusiastic notes. Those conceits, Mr. Williamson thinks, are basically different from the one he so admires in "To the Countesse of

Denbigh." For these wilder flights of fancy he blames Marino. And yet those conceits which Mr. Williamson and many others have attacked as merely ingenious, purely decorative, grotesque or perverse, are in fact emblems just as truly as the example analyzed above. Failure to perceive this fact is perhaps the factor chiefly responsible for those numerous and gross misapprehensions which abound in critical studies.

"On the Bleeding Wounds of Our Crucified Lord," which Odette de Mourgues has singled out for special condemnation, will furnish a general example of an image used emblematically.[3] In typical Baroque fashion, Crashaw fixes his attention on the sensuous object, the bleeding wounds, for the purpose of rising through this contemplation to the full significance of the crucifixion. In the fourth stanza he exclaims:

> But o thy side! thy deepe dig'd side
> That hath a double Nilus going,

Nilus is an excellent example of an image used as a *contracted* emblem. Just as the Nile, by overflowing its banks, enriches the arid land, bringing forth crops and fruits, so the precious blood of Christ sanctifies, making possible the life of grace. In short, the doctrine of mankind's redemption through Christ's passion and death has been compressed into this image.

On the basis of the poem in question it is already possible to make several generalizations concerning the nature of Crashaw's emblematic imagery, generalizations which will be progressively strengthened as this study proceeds. Much has been said of the sensuous nature of Crashaw's imagery, and one can hardly deny that his images are indeed more sensuous and more *inherently* emotional than Donne's. Still, this generalization can be lethal unless one adds two qualifications.

First, by far the most important thing to notice in the two lines quoted above is that a Christian doctrine has been embodied in the *Nilus* image: the image is the sign of a concept. The second qualification is not so easily demonstrated. The *Nilus* image, even though not a traditional Christian symbol, is probably not intended to be visualized in all its particulars. I doubt that we are expected to conjure up a detailed Nile scene complete with reeds, Ibis, and crocodile. A deep response is doubtless intended, but it is on the concept embodied more than on any sensuous particular that our attention should be riveted.

Extravagant ornamentation, lush, detailed development is perhaps what comes to the minds of most readers when the poetry of Crashaw is mentioned. This embellishment is an important aspect of his poetry, but Crashaw frequently succeeds in packing into a narrow framework a good deal of thought. It is precisely here, in the use of the contracted emblem, that the connection between Crashaw and the "schools" of Donne and Jonson is most clearly perceived. The contracted emblem, packed with thought, clearly owes much to the Donnean and Herbertian tradition; the epigrammatic terseness and exquisite cadence with which these contracted emblems are given verbal expression are more reminiscent of Jonson and Carew than of Spenser or the Elizabethan lyricists.

In perhaps no Crashaw poem is it so essential for the modern reader to keep in mind this conceptual basis of the imagery as in "Blessed Be the Paps which Thou Hast Sucked":

> Suppose He had been tabled at thy teats,
> Thy hunger feels not what He eats:
> He'll have His teat ere long, a bloody one—
> The mother then must suck the Son.

For Robert Adams this poem comes close to being a "revolting joke on Jesus and Mary," with horrible suggestions of "incest and perversion." [4]

Things are not really so exciting as all that, although from most readers such a reaction is inevitable. Basic to the meaning of the epigram is the symbolic use of physical feeding for spiritual nourishment.[5] The prose "meaning" of the poem is that although during His infancy Christ was dependent upon His mother for food (physical sustenance), she, to be redeemed, depended upon the shedding of His precious blood during the Crucifixion (spiritual sustenance). This meaning emerges even more clearly when one remembers that *blood* is the symbol of God's redemptive act; hence, of divine love.

Still, this symbolical interpretation does not explain why the poet has insisted upon focusing the readers' attention on what are to most people highly unwelcome particulars. The genre (epigram) with its emphasis on antithetical point is responsible here. Basically, the paradox is *conceptual*: the Blessed Virgin, who nourished Christ with milk, was in turn redeemed by His Blood, shed upon the cross. But partly to achieve sharpness of point, this basically intellectual paradox has been rendered in highly concrete form. The resulting surprise is intentional, for the main purpose of the religious epigram, which typically employs either conceit or paradox, is to startle the reader into contemplation of a religious truth. In modern terms, the religious epigrammist sought at all cost to avoid a "stock response." What oft was thought but ne'er so cleverly expressed was his chief purpose.

If this particular epigram horrifies the modern reader rather than pleasantly startles him into a new consideration of old truths, it is chiefly because he is not accustomed to reacting to an image *exclusively* for its value as a symbol. Typically, it is hard for him entirely to divorce an image from its literal meaning. But during the seventeenth century the tendency to image thought and feeling was at its height, and nowhere was this more true than in religious poetry.

Mr. Adams' reference to the "extra incongruity" of "Tabled at thy Teates"—Crashaw's sudden injection of a homely word amid spiritual reflections—lays a finger on an element common in Crashaw's poetry and, in fact, not rare in Donne's. The juxtaposition of the sacred and profane, of the celestial and the lowly is familiar to the reader of medieval religious works. One should recall that the lines which since the eighteenth century have so rigidly divided the sacred from the profane, the celestial from the lowly, the serious from the jocose, were just beginning to be drawn during Crashaw's time. And the men who were most eager to draw them and insist upon them were those with whom our poet had least in common. That which strikes us as bizarre incongruity is really nothing more than the final sparks of one element of the medieval religious tradition which (like several other elements in this tradition) burned with peculiar brilliance just before being extinguished. It is too sanguine to hope that this interpretation will bring about the sudden popularity of "Blessed Be the Paps Which Thou Hast Sucked," but the explanation offered here will perhaps remove the necessity of charging to Crashaw's credit unspeakable perversions or blasphemous jokes.

Not all of Crashaw's verbal emblems are so displeasing to modern taste. In "A Hymn of the Nativity" the two shepherds address the Christ Child:

> We saw Thee in Thy balmy nest,
> Young dawn of our eternal day;
> We saw thine eyes break from the East,
> And chase the trembling shades away.

With lines such as these the danger for the modern reader is that his response will be *incomplete*. Charmed by the loveliness of the imagery, he may rest only half aware of the thoughts embodied therein. These four lines pierce through the very core of the meaning of the Incarnation and to this traditional dogma they give an expression at once imagistic and remarkably succinct. The Christ Child is the "young dawn of our eternal day." The comparison of the natural light and warmth of the earthly sun with the divine light and warmth radiating from the Son of God is a favorite one of Crashaw's. The Divine Son is the source of love and intellectual activity, and the cause of spiritual life, just as the earthly sun is the source of physical warmth and light and the cause of natural life. The verbal pun enhances the appeal of the analogy. Day, like light, has a variety of symbolic meanings with Crashaw as it does with Vaughan. All these meanings, though, are related, referring always to something numinous. To Crashaw the *day* or fullness of light refers sometimes to the mystical life, extraordinary illumination; sometimes (as in the case in question) *day* refers to the state of grace, whereby the Christian is united to Christ in faith, hope, and love. The cause of this state of grace, the culmination of which is the Beatific Vision (thus, "eternal day") is Christ's redemptive love, first revealed at the Incarnation—just as the cause of the physical light of day is the sun, first visible at dawn. In the last two lines the eyes of the Christ Child (the dawning sun) become the East (which in turn points to the richly suggestive Rising Sun), and the light from the opening eyes chases away the trembling shades. Here in a nutshell is the second half of Milton's *Nativity Ode*. The material world, formerly in bondage to Satan, has been redeemed; the power of darkness has been broken; evil forces retreat, for

Christ has wrought the reconciliation of the material and spiritual, lost since Adam's sin.

All the above has been stated in four terse lines of complex theological symbolism. The symbols themselves are traditional enough, but their juxtaposition for the expression of a highly specific meaning demanded by the poem is a matter of Crashaw's own ingenious devising. What is especially worthy of note is that the emblematic picture of the last two lines proceeds almost logically from the first two lines; there is no apparently careless gliding of image to image. The last lines are, of course, a conceit, but one so energized by the emotion of the whole that it deserves to be called poetic insight.

Of all Crashaw's symbols, the richest in application is the Phoenix, an outstanding example of which occurs in the third line of the eighth stanza of this same hymn: "The Phoenix builds the phoenix' nest." In spite of the medieval Bestiary tradition, the Phoenix does not seem to have been often used in Renaissance poetry. Yet the points of analogy are many. The Phoenix and Christ are both unique. The Phoenix is sacred to the sun, a common symbol for Christ. The home of the Phoenix is in the East (with the suggestion of the Rising Sun), where, upon growing old, this Arabian bird builds itself a spicy nest, is burned alive, but rises with renewed life from the ashes. The application to the Resurrection is obvious. Like the Phoenix, Christ has built his own nest (that is, God the Father has created the Blessed Virgin). Indirectly, this verbal emblem pays a magnificent compliment to the Virgin Mary, for the nest of the Phoenix is richly aromatic, symbolical even in the Old Testament of acceptability to God.

The emblem obviously encourages intellectual ingenuity. Perhaps the peak of Crashaw's intellectual complexity is reached in the last stanzas of that magnificent ode "Hymn to the Name above Every Name" and yet without sacrifice of his gift for rhapsodical music. (Only lines 216–219 are quoted here.)

> What *did* their Weapons but sett wide the Doores
> For thee: Fair, purple Doores of love's devising;
> The Ruby windowes which inrich't the EAST
> Of Thy so oft repeated rising.

In these four lines a wealth of theological doctrine has been embodied. Unwittingly, the executioners serve Christ's ends, for through their cruelty the martyr achieves a magnificent spiritual triumph, meriting that crown which repays him immeasurably for this suffering. Moreover, the heroic fortitude displayed by the victim is eloquent testimony of the power of Christ, Whose grace has made such constancy possible. For this reason the doors are "fair." The windows are *ruby* not only because they are red, but because the blood of martyrs is *precious* even beautiful in the sight of God. In another sense, they are precious to the martyr too, since they are both an opportunity for the expression of his love and a sign of the eternal reward about to be bestowed.

These fair, purple doors are said, paradoxically, to be of *love's* devising. Much thought has been packed away into this word. Christ, through His love, has permitted this martyrdom for the spiritual benefit of the victim, who (according to Catholic dogma) gains complete remission of sin and immediate entry into heaven; and perhaps for the spiritual benefit of all men, that Christians might be edified and strengthened by such an example of fortitude and that the pagans might be attracted to the Christian faith. *Love's* may also refer to the martyr himself, since his wounds are the most eloquent testimony to his fidelity. Then there is the restatement of these concepts in the clause "which enrich't the East of Thy so oft repeated Rising," *The East,* of course, referring to Christ (the Rising Sun). It is hoped that even this brief analysis will make the reader reluctant to accept Mrs. Bennett's verdict. Speaking of the very passage quoted above, she tells us that "The intellect is operative, not before or after, but only in the moment of apprehending the image." [6] And later, referring to several passages, the above quoted lines being one of them, she concludes that "the function of the intellect in Crashaw's poetry is to justify an unusual collocation of sensations." [7]

It is no less wrong to see in such a passage an exemplification of Crashaw's masochism. Surely *triumph* rather than masochism describes the spirit of this passage, the triumph of a love (both human and divine) powerful enough to transform even the most horrid butchery into an immediate victory, powerful enough to utilize the most barbarous crime for the glorification of God and as a vehicle of grace for both the martyr and his fellow men. Much of what has been written off as Crashaw masochism appears to be nothing more melodramatic than rather traditional Christian symbolism and attitudes.

It must be admitted, though, that the unity of opposites (pain and pleasure in this case) sometimes induces a sense of strain or even grotesqueness. Perhaps Mr. Adams is correct in concluding that it is precisely because Crashaw succeeds so well in unifying to one assertion, even over the most intense opposition, elements which most of us prefer to keep quite separate, that contemporary taste is sometimes repelled and sometimes amused by him. Readers can indeed argue from such a passage as the one quoted from "Carmen Deo Nostro" that Crashaw was masochistic or psychotic—but only if they choose to ignore the concepts expressed through his imagery.

The implications of this view of Crashaw's imagery are far-reaching. The root cause of the common modern failure to appreciate Baroque poetry (even among those who claim to understand the aim of the Baroque writer) is a misreading of the imagery. By this, much more is implied than a failure to recognize traditional symbols and emblems for what they are. Some readers visualize the images too vividly; they dwell too long on the concrete elaborations. Where the poet expects them to meditate or at least to grasp a concept, they remain immersed in sensuous particulars. Mario Praz complains that far too often the Baroque poet ended up by materializing the spiritual rather than spiritualizing the temporal, but perhaps modern readers rather than Baroque poets are guilty.

But it is not Crashaw's contracted emblems which give modern readers the most trouble. Far more formidable stumbling blocks are those rather extended emblems which involve elaborate ornamentation, those which we have come to regard as most typically (or notoriously) Baroque. The twentieth century has never been kind to ornamentation. Most modern readers regard it as a mere superimposition, something basically irrelevant; they may well ask how such ornamentation (as they think they have read in Crashaw) is to be harmonized with the contemplation of a concept. It is profitable to inspect Crashaw's own view of ornamentation, expressed in this passage from our poet's address to his tutor Lany, which comprises the preface to the *Epigrammata Sacra* of 1634:

> Nor assuredly than this kind of writing, provided it have sufficiently discharged its proper functions, could anything be more suitable to theological leisure; for in it without doubt the very substance of theology being overlaid with poetic grace, sets off its grandeur by loveliness.[8]

Commenting on this passage, Miss White reminds us that the ornament is not something superimposed, merely affixed, but "something immediately relevant that brings out the meaning of the thing ornamented and awakens the mind to an appreciation of it." [9] In fact, among Renaissance rhetoricians, the word *ornament* is practically synonymous with *delight*.

It is interesting that Crashaw, like Pierfrancesco Minozzi, assumes that imagistic richness and elaboration is most suitable precisely in the type of writing where modern taste usually demands simplicity—the religious poem. Even the contemporary Puritans saw nothing incompatible between metaphorical richness and sincere religious utterance. And doctrinal exposition by means of elaborate imagistic development is not without Biblical precedent. The student of seventeenth-century religious poetry would do well to grant more than passing notice to the imagist complexity of some of St. Paul's passages; to this one, for instance: "Epistle to the Romans," Ch. XI. Hebraic simplicity should be made of sterner stuff. Had Crashaw dared to express the same thoughts with the same imagery, we would be hearing even now of sexual inhibitions, vicarious enjoyment, guilt complexes. Crashaw's case is especially complex, for it is next to impossible, ordinarily, to draw a sharp line between Biblical influence and that of the Jesuit epigrammatic tradition.

The second class of emblematic images is the *extended* or *embellished* type. It is the attitude toward these richly ornamented images which our book hopes to readjust. Unfriendly critics have written these images off as redundancy of a peculiarly obnoxious sort. Crashaw's friendlier critics have generally granted the redundancy of the embellished images, but have described them as esthetically pleasing nonetheless. This alleged redundancy they have excused as warranted by the need for dramatic emphasis, rhetorical repetition, or

luxurious amplitude. This analysis hopes to demonstrate that
Crashaw's imagistic embellishments (unlike those of, say,
Marino) are rarely redundant or *purely* iterative; typically,
they subtly but significantly advance the developing thought.
This is a thesis which, we believe, bears important implications for the interpretation of Crashaw. However, the present
chapter will develop this thesis only briefly and partially;
the heart of the argument will be delayed until the third
chapter, which analyzes Crashaw's most notorious "lush and
redundant" images. The justification for this annoying delay
is that the argument cannot be persuasively developed unless
the reader has before him the information offered in the
second chapter.

The study of Crashaw's contracted emblems commenced
with an analysis of the fourth stanza of "On the Bleeding
Wounds of Our Crucified Lord." The fifth stanza is a good
example of the type of verbal emblem classified as *extended*:

> Water'd by the showres they bring,
> The thornes that thy blest browes encloses
> (A cruel and costly spring)
> Conceive proud hopes of proving roses.

The comments of a perceptive critic deserve attention.
Mr. Alvarez sees in these lines a "Perverse logic of ornamentation." It is perfectly clear, he maintains, *how* Crashaw arrives
at any given line, but it is hard to see *why* he arrives there.
This, he suggests, is what T. S. Eliot meant when he charged
Crashaw with perversity.[10] It should be admitted immediately
that this critic is keenly aware of the basically intellectual
nature of Crashaw's imagery. He knows there is "brainwork"
afoot; but why, he wonders, this particular emblem? This
is a fair question, and one which (it seems certain) Mr. Al-

varez and many other critics would ask of certain other, far more objectionable passages. One answers this hypothetical question by asserting that the particular image is there because of the *conceptual exigencies* of the poem. With extraordinary terseness, the preceding stanza announces the redemptive power of the bloody passion. Logically following from this dogma (logic of *thought*, not of image) is the *preciousness* of Christ's blood. Now, it is this thought which Crashaw embodies in another and far more sensuous emblem. Specifically, that the blood and sweat of Christ are in themselves sacred and of miraculous power has been expressed by prosopopeia (the attributing of human emotions to inanimate objects), while the parenthetical "cruel and costly spring" calls our attention to the horror of the situation.

Mr. Alvarez has admitted the logic involved in the particulars of the imagistic ornamentation. What this study insists upon is that the "ingenious logic of ornamentation" follows in perfectly parallel fashion the logical development of the meditative thought. Each detail of ornamentation corresponds to a concept. Image glides into image just as thought glides into thought, although, admittedly, the poet does not strive for terseness in these embellished emblems. The poet seems to be striving, rather, for opulence and abundance—certainly his privilege.

But what is to be said to a reader who, even though admitting all the above, objects to this method of expression per se? Only this: *de gustibus non est disputandum.* The situation alters, though, when the professional critic enters upon the scene. He is asked to refrain from value judgments based *solely* upon personal taste. It is easy to regard such taste as axiomatic when it is shared by almost all of one's contemporaries.

An unusual example both of embellishment and of rhetor-

ical emphasis achieved imagistically comprises the greater
part of the epigram "To Pontius Pilate washing his blood-
stained Hands," one of two such passages among the "Divine
Epigrams":

> Is murder no sin? or a sin so cheap,
>> That thou need'st heap
> A rape upon't? till thy adult'rous touch
> Taught her these sullied cheeks, this blubber'd face.
> She was a nymph, the meadows knew none such,
>> Of honest parentage, of unstain'd race,
> The daughter of a fair and well-famed fountain,
> As ever silver-tipp'd the side of shady mountain.
> See how she weeps, and weeps, that she appears
>> Nothing but tears;
> Each drop's a tear that weeps for her own waste.
>> Hark, how at at every touch she does complain her!
> Hark, how she bids her frighted drops make haste,
> And with sad murmurs chides the hands that stain her!
> Leave, leave for shame, or else, good judge, decree,
> What water shall wash this, when this hath washed thee.

The mythological genealogy, the elaborate and poetically
effective prosopopeia, the many repetitive phrases and clauses
—all of these work together in cumulative fashion to produce one grand effect, the full realization of the horrendous
nature of Pilate's crime. These particulars are like so many
points comprising an emotional and imagistic route to a
basically cognitive goal. The elaboration proceeds according
to a definite plan, one well calculated to achieve this end.
First there is direct statement, then lengthy embellishment
to enhance and emphasize the statement and to prepare
emotionally for the next direct statement which will stand in
such violent contrast to what has gone before. Water was

once a pure nymph. But this direct statement does not suffice. The poet goes on to elaborate, to prepare the reader emotionally for what follows; the direct statement that the water has turned to tears is all the more impressive because it follows immediately upon the elaboration of limpidity and freshness. This emotional heightening, then, really serves the purposes of the poetic meditation.

Following the direct statement is an elaboration on the theme of the water's weeping. Crashaw makes skillful use of each particular (the rapid flow of the water and its murmurs) to underscore the water's sorrow and horror of contamination. Even this purifying element in the universe has been stained, so abominable are the polluting hands. The emotional effect of the passage is almost visceral; intentionally so, for this is a matter of *per sensus ad intellectum*.

This passage is not so typical of Crashaw as are the others studied this far, for it is obvious that the reader is expected to respond emotionally to each particular of the imagistic development, perhaps even to visualize it, and *then* to rise above this emotion to grasp a concept. Specifically, it seems that the reader is expected to shudder and even feel a visceral revulsion as pure water itself is irreparably stained—but as an aid to realizing more fully the horror of the crime. The chief purpose of the imagery in this epigram is to effect an emotional reaction; this emotional reaction, in turn, is used like an icon, to point to a spiritual concept. Ordinarily, the images of Crashaw are purely symbolic, pointing directly to a concept, the emotional response deriving from the concept embodied in the image rather than from the image itself.

It is not easy to classify the imagery of this epigram. One can hardly say that the images are actual visible symbols of ideas. On the other hand, although they do indeed elicit and control an emotional response, their ultimate purpose is so purely ideational that one hesitates calling this passage an example of Crashaw's symbolic allusiveness. Should the definition of emblem be extended to include such passages as these, which point to a clearly determinable concept without embodying one? Emblem, surely, is not the right word, but there is none. Literary scholarship still lacks a satisfactory system of imagistic classification as well as a truly definitive study of the nature of symbolic imagery.

In the epigram "Our Lord to His Father" we are back to the typical Crashaw method, in which images are actual visible symbols of ideas. In this poem the emblem is used to repeat a concept for purposes of amplification, with a striking crescendo-like effect. Christ has told His Father that if He likes the taste of these few drops of blood shed at the Circumcision, He will soon be granted a whole sea of it. This notion is developed:

> Thy wrath that wades here now ere long shall swim,
> The flood-gate shall be set open wide for him.
> Then let him drink and drink and do his worst,
> To drown the wantonness of his wild thirst.

The same type of amplification occurs at the end of the poem. The tiny wounds are regarded as adumbrations of the mortal ones:

> These purple buds of blooming death may be
> Erst the full stature of a fatal tree:

Immediately the notion is amplified, for dramatic emphasis, in the last two lines of the epigram:

> And, till my riper woes to age are come,
> This knife may be the spear's praeludium.

The most lavish use of the emblem for purposes of repetition in Baroque poetry is a twenty-five line passage from "To the Name Above Every Name, the Name of Jesus. A Hymn." Image after image arises to express the richness and the treasure embodied in the name *Jesus*. The psalmist was content with "Taste and see how sweet the Lord is," but Crashaw develops and enriches as if he were attempting to convey the *infinite extent* of the sweetness and goodness. However, the reader with a sound knowledge of traditional symbols (for example, *Arabias, frankincense, myrrh, spices*) will recognize that each iterative image subtly advances the thought.

We might do well to propose some general observations on ornamentation in Crashaw's poetry, for it is this aspect of the Baroque which causes most readers great difficulty. The attempt to draw a sharp line between Spenserian pictorial fluidity and what we call the Baroque does not lie within the scope of this study. Mr. Moloney has made the best start, but only that. He observes that Baroque luxuriance is not embellishment of both line and image as with Spenser, but of image alone.[11] For the present this study wishes merely to propose for discussion this hypothesis: that Baroque luxuriance has its roots in the Spenserian poetic method. It is not necessary to posit Marino's poetry as the *prime* source of Crashaw's embellishments, although its influence was substantial. But Spenserian ornamentation was affected by four forces which profoundly altered it: the Jonsonian tradition, which affected the luxuriance or embellishment of line (not image) —by trimming it; that growing intellectuality so characteristic of early seventeenth-century English culture, which tied ornamentation much more tightly to thought than it had been, although embellishment, even with Spenser, is not usually totally divorced from meaning; certain methods of formal meditation (especially the Ignatian and the Salesian) which had become popular in England by the early seventeenth century; and, paradoxically, the dissolution of the medieval world picture and the medieval manner of thinking. In early seventeenth-century England it was possible for the first time to look upon material objects in a manner *exclusively* "scientific" or "objective," but it was still possible to regard these same objects as analogues of spiritual realities. These symbols, however, no longer enjoyed a secure place in a grand, perfectly coherent allegorical scheme. They existed, for the most part, as individual fragments. This fragmentary existence, it is tempting to suggest, was necessary before such symbols could serve the poet as instruments of contemplation or psychological analysis.

Speaking of Baroque ornamentation in art and poetry, Mr. Sypher remarks that Baroque piety is able to "consolidate and fulfill experience at the level of the flesh, if the image is sufficiently powerful." The crisis in the mannerist conscience can be resolved in the external, material world. After the tensions of high Gothic art there was a moment of *détente*, during which the spiritual became fleshy.[12] Speaking of Baroque literature, one may regard these last two assertions as dangerous exaggerations without denying that the Baroque religious poet does show greater willingness than most poets to embody spiritual truths in sensuous images. A typical Crashaw poem surely merits such terms as "redundance," "abundance," "körperlichkeit" (provided these are properly understood). Especially applicable to Crashaw's more ornamented emblems is Wölffin's apt phrase "Die Freude in der Stoffgewalt."[13] Undeniably, the Baroque poet takes joy in the power of his icon, in working with materiality. And there is a tendency towards generous amplification and repetition which even the meditative purpose of the lyrics does not completely explain. The parallel between pictorial arts and poetry such as Crashaw's is drawn with justification if based on the qualities mentioned above. One cannot avoid asking why both religious poetry and religious art of the period are charac- terized by generous amplification and imagistic realization of concepts. Perhaps the general crisis in conscience and faith is responsible. The assurance of the senses and grand effects were sought to resolve uncertainties.

The last characteristic of Crashaw's ornamentation to be discussed here has been aptly described by Mr. Alvarez, who points to the element of "vigorous enjoyment in the writing itself." [14] The Baroque poet does, in fact, take rather open delight not only in materiality but also in the very process of embellishing and in the skillful use of rhetorical devices. Few if any critics have suggested that this innocent, almost child- ish joy may be much akin to the spirit of le jongleur de Notre Dame. Just as the juggler offers his lowly skill to the honor and glory of God, so the Baroque poet "performs" out of reverence, offering his talent up to God. This is a hard saying for moderns, biased as they are in favor of whatever seems spontaneous and "natural." Somehow, they associate with reverence "simplicity" or speechlessness, surely not rhetorical pyrotechnics.

Thus it seems that for several reasons the *Zeitgeist* rather than alleged Protestant aggression is Crashaw's most formid- able foe. The new critic, one recalls, may hold suspect a method of poetic analysis which relies on historical back- ground even to the extent the present study does. Actually, if our minds, as they read a Crashaw poem, were really *tab- ulae rasae,* something might be said for a "new critic" ap- proach to Crashaw. But no mature mind can be that. For example, Mr. Empson, even if he has ignored the seven- teenth-century intellectual milieu, has surely not succeeded in ignoring his own. He has dispensed with meditative manuals and Counter-Reformation theology, but unfortunately, not with Freud. It is foolish to suppose that any reader can divorce a literary work from its cultural surroundings. Whether the reader wishes to or not, he will in fact set the art object down squarely into a cultural milieu, either into its *proper* context, or into his own contemporary one.

In short, what we bring to a reading of Crashaw are minds in which lurk all the esthetic assumptions of the last two centuries. These last two hundred years have taught us (among many other things which hamper a genuine appreciation of Crashaws poetry) to associate sensuous particulars with emotion, mood, or even attitude perhaps—hardly ever with clear concepts. No poet requires of the reader a more strenuous orientation of responses than does Crashaw.

As this study has shown, the emblem in Crashaw's poetry appears in a variety of types and serves several functions, although all are basically intellectual. But critical literature has nowhere pointed out, much less studied, a type of verbal emblem which Crashaw devises with unusual skill. One of his specialties is using traditional symbols as building blocks for complex emblems. One such emblematic picture is the following from "A Hymn to the Name and Honour of the Admirable Saint Theresa." St. Teresa's soul at the moment of death is—

> Like a soft lump of incense, hasted
> By too hot a fire, and wasted
> Into perfuming clouds, so fast
> Shalt thou exhale to heaven at last
> In a resolving sigh.

The key images comprising this emblem are all traditional symbols: incense symbolizes consecration to God; the hot fire

symbolizes spiritual ardor; the perfume stands for acceptability to God. Teresa, consecrated to God, dies because of excessive spiritual ardor (Neoplatonic notion) and enjoys
forever the Beatific Vision. All of this has been expressed by
means of an emblematic picture constructed from three traditional symbols.

This remarkable skill in matching imagistic and logical
interrelationships is—at least to some extent—the fruit of
emblem reading, an activity quite remote from our experience. Crashaw, however, takes for granted an intimate
acquaintance with emblem books. In fact, the epigram "On
the Baptized Ethiopian" (Let it no longer be a forlorn hope,/
To wash an Ethiope") loses much of its point unless the
reader knows that a standard emblematic representation of
the immutability of nature was the picture of two men
vainly trying to scrub an African white. Whitney uses such
an emblem plate with the motto "Nature cannot be changed":
"Leave of with paine, the blackamore to showre,/With wash-
ings ofte, and wipings more than due." [15]

The tracing of some of Crashaw's emblematic images to
possible sources in emblem books current in the England of
his day will not only serve to substantiate the central thesis
of this chapter but should also shed some needed light on the
religious temper of the times. We shall see, for example, that
a considerable number of good Protestants were meditating
on those "un-English" emblem plates which some modern
critics have labeled as predominantly continental and Catholic.

One must keep in mind, though, the special difficulty encountered in tracing Crashaw's emblematic images. The
Newberry Library in Chicago possesses one of the most remarkable collections of emblem literature in the United
States, but even this splendid collection contains barely a

third of the emblem books described in Mario Praz's bibliography. Nor does even Praz's invaluable list represent all the emblem books extant in Renaissance Europe, more than a few of which are forever lost to us. In short, present inability to trace a given emblematic image to a specific emblem plate is surely no proof that no such source existed or may not yet exist.

The emblematic pattern of most of Crashaw's imagery is the key to its most disturbing features. The source of Crashaw's nest and breast imagery has long puzzled scholars. In the next chapter I suggest a passage from St. Francis de Sales as a possible source, but also worthy of serious consideration is an emblem of van Haeften's, entitled "Azylum Cordis in Latere Vulnerato" (Asylum of the Heart in the Wounded Side).[16] Divine Love (who appears as Cupid in all the emblems under consideration here) is stretched out on the cross, a dove's nest on his right breast, on which Anima (who has climbed a ladder) gazes lovingly. The motto under the emblem plate reads "Esto quasi columba nidificans in summo ore foraminis" (Be like the dove which nests). The meditation on this emblem shows that the nest constructed on the breast of Christ symbolizes the security and rewards of God's love, in which the pure of heart will find comfort.

Among the images in Crashaw's poetry which modern readers find most distasteful are those in which olfactory or gustatory processes are prominent, especially when the substance to be tasted is blood. But if we are to judge the taste of Crashaw's contemporaries by the emblems which they seem to have most enjoyed, we must conclude that they would have found nothing to disturb them in Crashaw. A popular emblem of the times is the wine press, one which Quarles reproduced.[17] Divine Love permits Himself to be crushed in a press. From His heart and hands streams of blood gush forth and flow, as wine, through a spout at the bottom of the press. Anima, joyous and eager, is lying prone, catching the wine-blood in a heart-shaped jug. In *Schola Cordis* Anima holds up a heart-shaped jug to Divine Love, who drinks from it joyously.[18] The meditation on this emblem informs us that the liquid which Christ drinks so eagerly is the penitence and love of the sinner. Unlike the wicked Jews who gave Christ gall to drink, the contrite sinner refreshes Him with the water of penitence and love, water which will spring into life eternal. When Christ said to the Samaritan woman, "Give me to drink," he really desired, the emblematist assures us, to taste of her penitence and love. (In "The Weeper," one recalls, the tears of the Magdalen are the angels' wine and the Master's water.)

In *Amoris Divini et Humani Effectus* a sick woman falls at the feet of Christ, holds up to him an empty cup into which gushes water from the Savior's side. The motto under the emblem plate reads, "Qui sanat infirmitates tuas" (He who heals your ailments).[19] Often reproduced in seventeenth-century emblem books is Hugo's emblem plate depicting Divine Love dragging Anima with a long rope. He is holding out a large jar from which emanate fragrant vapors. Intoxicated by these, Anima has swooned and stretches out her hands helplessly, languorously, toward the fragrant perfumes.[20] The motto reads, not surprisingly, "Trahe me— post te curremus in odorem unguentorum tuorum. Cant. I." (Drag me—we shall run after you, following the fragrance of your ointments.)

In spite of Alciati's occasional borrowing from medieval bestiary material (1534), animal and plant symbolism is not common in sixteenth-century English and continental religious poetry. It was Joachim Camerarius (Chambrier) who played the leading role in bringing into fashion again the symbolism of the medieval bestiaries. Collecting materials from Pliny, Appianus, and Aelianus, this physician published, in Nuremberg, from 1590 to 1604, four emblem books, for which materials were drawn, respectively, from plants, from quadrupeds, from birds and insects, and from fishes, amphibians, and reptiles.[21] These are far richer in materials than the medieval *Physiologus* (republished in Rome, 1587). One cannot miss the influence of these popular and widely circulating emblem books on subsequent emblematic literature both continental and English. There is, after the publication of Camerarius' works, a clearly noticeable increase in animal and plant symbolism both in emblem books and in English devotional literature.

Crashaw uses animal symbolism oftener than does any other English devotional poet. In fact, the preoccupation with bizarre images which has characterized most of Crashaw's critics has obscured the fact that animal symbols play a leading role in much of Crashaw's best poetry. The self-sacrificing pelican and the phoenix, which Crashaw uses so skillfully, are the animals most frequently encountered in emblem books. Indeed, few emblem books of the time lack them.[22] Eagles and eaglets are also frequently employed in the emblem literature; Crashaw uses them to represent St. Teresa and her followers, respectively. Crashaw's third volume (*Symbolorum & Emblematum ex Volatilibus et Insectis desumtorum centuria tertia collecta*) treats the reader to more than a dozen eagle emblems, in all of which the eagle symbolizes either lofty virtue or saintly aspirants to mysticism. The Puritan Andrew Willet, whose popular emblem book seems to have escaped the attention of most scholars, borrowed freely from Camerarius. Willet presents an eagle soaring into sublime heights, looking down with scorn upon worldly preoccupations; neither lightning nor mountains succeed in frightening it as it soars ever higher.[23] In another emblem foolish crows try to worry the eagle, which ignores them. The crows are worldly men who try vainly to tempt the saintly man to abandon his quest for spiritual perfection. In emblem No. 9 a huge eagle is pictured carrying its progeny to the sun, for it is the nature of the eagle to teach its young to love the sun and aspire to lofty heights. This is why, Willet tells us, St. John the Apostle was represented as an eagle. Again, in emblem No. 11, the eagle is depicted teaching its young to fly from the nest. As was shown much earlier, Crashaw seems to have made use of all this rich symbolism. The eagle seldom occurs in religious devotional poetry, even though it was reproduced often enough in emblem books, after Camerarius. George Wither provides us with an interesting example of a reproduction of one of Camerarius' plates: an eaglet is perched on a winged ball, which in turn rests on an altar. On each side serpents unsuccessfully attack the bird.[24] Virtue aspires to sublime heights and is indifferent both to earthly blessings, which it sees as ephemeral and fickle (hence the winged ball) and to the attacks of worldlings.

Neither the lamb nor the dove appears in the emblem literature as often as we should expect, but Camerarius prepared more than twenty emblems for each (in volumes II and III respectively). Crashaw's application of the dove symbol is unusually rich, as George Williams has demonstrated. Camerarius' third volume is a possible source. One can easily find parallels there for all the symbolic meanings which Williams has assigned to Crashaw's many uses of the dove symbol.

If asked to select the Crashaw image which is most disturbing to modern readers, one would most likely single out the concluding line of the epigram "Blessed be the Paps which thou hast Sucked": "Then must the mother suck the son." The sucking of breasts is not uncommonly depicted in emblem books of the time. The ultimate source, surely is the Song of Songs, "Thy breasts are better than honey" (Cant. 4:10), the motto for an interesting emblem in *Amoris Divini et Humani Effectus,* in which Anima is shown sucking the breast of Divine Love.[25] One of Quarles' emblems—and let us keep in mind that he adapted continental emblem material for use of Protestants—is grosser. His emblem plate (for which I cannot find a source) depicts an enormous breast.[26] A bloated, pig-faced man is sucking the left teat (rather too graphically delineated for the tastes of many) while a woman is milking the right teat. The motto (Isaiah 66:2) reads, "Ye may suck, but not be satisfied with the breast of her consolation." This emblem book was especially popular among Nonconformists. Let us read the first two stanzas of Quarles' poem to see what was considered proper reading fare for good Protestants of those days:

> What never fill'd? Be thy lips screw'd so fast
>> To th'earth's full breast? For shame, for shame un-
>> seize thee;
> Thou takest a surfeit where thou should'st but taste,
>> And mak'st too much not half enough to please thee.
>> Ah, fool, forbear; thou swallowest at one breath
>> Both food and poison down! thou draw'st both milk
>> and death.
>
> The ub'rous breasts, when fairly drawn, repast
>> The thriving infant, with their milky flood,
> But being overstrain'd, return at last,
>> Unwholesome gulps composed of wind and blood.
>> A mod'rate use does both repast and please;
> Who strains beyond a mean, draws in and gulps disease.

Seventeenth-century English Protestants, it seems, failed to realize that such imagery was thoroughly un-English; for so great was the popularity of Quarles' emblem book that forty years after its debut the work had already run through a dozen editions.

The next chapter will discuss Crashaw's indebtedness to St. Teresa of Avila and St. Francis de Sales for the wound of love images, especially for the reciprocal wounding; but emblem books abound with darts of love, woundings with arrows, and delicious, languorous deaths, especially Hugo's *Pia Desideria* and Quarles' adaptations of Hugo's emblems. One might single out as a fairly commonly reproduced emblem of the early seventeenth century the reciprocal wound. Anima and Divine Love have shot an arrow through each other's heart and gaze rapturously at each other. The motto reads, "Sit in amore Reciprocitas." (Let there be reciprocity in love.) What we are witnessing, obviously, is the graphic representation of the wound of love imagery. Another representative example of this type of emblem, so common in the second and third decades of the seventeenth century, is this one from the widely circulated *Amoris Divini et Humani Effectus*. Graphically representing the motto "Vulnerasti cor meum, soror mea sponsa" (Cant. 4:9) (You have wounded my heart, my sister, my bride.) is a picture of Divine Love with pierced, bleeding heart exposed, at which Anima clutches eagerly.[27] An especially interesting example of the type of sensibility with which we are dealing is an emblem whose Pauline motto reads, "Cum Christo confixus sum cruci." [28] (With Christ I am nailed to the cross.) Divine Love is preparing to nail Anima to the cross with Him, driving a nail through her hand. The bodies intertwine; Anima is enraptured.

By far the most frequently employed symbol in the

seventeenth-century emblem books (though hardly ever encountered in the late sixteenth century) is the heart. Many
emblem books, both English and continental, present the
heart in numerous employments, all corresponding to some
spiritual state. For instance, Quarles, drawing upon Hugo's
Pia Desideria, shows us a heart burning and smoking on an
altar, being crushed with a pestle, bleeding profusely after
being pierced by an arrow, crowned with thorns, producing
a crop of lovely flowers, and in many other dramatic situa-
tions.[29]

Also influential on the development of Crashaw's poetic
style was a new type of devotional book developed largely
by the Jesuits in the first three or four decades of the seventeenth century. These new books joined the function of the
Emblem Book with that of the traditional devotional man-
ual, presenting a series of meditations on a single religious
topic by means of emblematic pictures and ingenious analyses
of these. Such is the procedure of the English Jesuit Henry
Hawkins, whose *Partheneia Sacra,* printed in English, in
1633, circulated widely in England, and not only among
Catholics. Like the other Catholic Emblem Book in England
(*The Devout Hart*) the *Parthenia Sacra* was written for a
Marian Sodality. In *Partheneia Sacra* the Marian meditations
are given an effective unity by the central, controlling
symbol, the garden, with its community of twenty-four
images, most of them flowers, analyzed with scientific mi-
nuteness. Of course, the bias is non-naturalistic, for the
detailed descriptions are merely the gathering of material for
emblematic pictures. Each detail, however minute, symbolizes
some attribute of the Virgin Mary. Hawkins' work is the only
example which comes to mind of an English work that sets
up a complex, formal meditation on a *single* religious topic
entirely by emblematic means. Unlike the English Protestant

Emblem Books, the work of Hawkins consists not of a succession of emblems on loosely related topics, but of a series of emblematic pictures which are logically related concepts in a formal meditation. There are more striking examples of complex imagistic analysis for purely emblematic purposes. In Hawkins we detect an obvious desire to decorate, but no particularization is ever anything other than a preparation for a meditation in symbolic mode. The climax of book is the "bridal" Assumption. Crashaw's poem on the Assumption, elaborated out of the May-morning lyric, has obvious connections with this emblem book.

An exhaustive study of emblematic sources for Crashaw's images cannot be attempted here. Nothing more is being attempted than a brief survey of some of the emblems which may have influenced Crashaw, but several other emblems are worth describing. Their possible relationship to Crashaw's images will be apparent immediately to anyone who has read the poet recently. A favorite emblem is the rapturous embrace of Anima and Divine Love; [30] the favorite emblematic method of representing spiritual aspiration is through wing symbolism. For instance, Quarles presents Anima sprouting wings, about to take flight into the heavens, where Divine Love beckons.[31] Wither, in several emblems, represents God's grace as sunlight,[32] and the same author offers his readers an emblem depicting the mutual love of saint and God. Two lighted tapers extend toward each other, almost touching. Just between and slightly above the two tapers is a large, flaming heart.[33]

One of Vaenius' emblems depicts the distillation of water. The emblematist explains that just as distilled water is a certain sign that fire is nearby, so tears guarantee the presence of the flame of love.[34] The same author presents the breast of Anima transfigured by rays proceeding from the eyes and halo of Divine Love. The motto reads "Mentis sol amor Dei." [35] (The sun of the mind is the love of God.) George Wither shows us a winged heart smoking profusely as it soars up to heaven. Thus the heart of the righteous seeks always for the things of God and will be ever perturbed (smoking) until it reaches heaven, its true home.[36] Beza's emblem book, one of several composed at Geneva, contains a picture of a gorgeous gem set in a ring. Thus, Beza tells us, does virtue shine, and goes on to elaborate this theme.[37]

One of Hugo's emblems has the motto, "Quis dabit capiti meo aquam et oculis meis fontem lacrymarum ut plorabo die ac nocte? Hierem. 9." (Who will give my head water and my eyes a fountain of tears so that I may weep day and night?) Anima sits before a fountain; from above, a nude Aquarius pours down water on her head. In the middle of a fountain stands a statue of a woman with hands extended, from which streams of water gush forth. Anima is weeping copiously.[38] Also deserving attention is the graphic representation of "Anima mea liquefacta est quando dilectus meus locutus est mihi" (Cant. 5:6). (My soul turned to water as my beloved spoke to me.) Anima is literally turning to water as the rays from the halo and eyes of Divine Love strike her body.[39]

In *Amoris Divini et Humani Effectus* Christ stands as the fountainhead, from whose hands, side, and feet water gushes to fill the large fountain basin, in which Anima washes a soiled heart. The motto admonishes the reader: "Lava a malitia cor tuum ut salvus fies. (Hierem. 4)" [40] (Wash your heart of all evil that you may be saved.) Vaenius presents an emblem with the motto "Amor docet." (Love teaches us.) From Divine Love, garbed as a university professor, streams of water gush forth, forming a pool; eagerly, students, on their hands and knees, lap it up.[41]

An emblem of Hugo's, frequently reproduced in later em-

blem books, should convince us that the playful preciosity of
the Baroque, for the contemporary reader at least, was by no
means incompatible with the expression of the most solemn,
sacred thoughts. The motto reads, "Quando veniam et ap-
parebo ante faciem Dei? Psal. 41." [42] (When shall I appear
before the face of God?) Anima, much distressed, is searching for Divine Love, who has hidden behind a drawn curtain,
much like a mischievous boy playing a prank on his mother.
He has several fingers in his mouth, and his eyes roll ever so
slightly in a roguish manner. The facial expression can be
described only as impishly precious and coy—or even "cute"
in the modern sense.

An emblem entitled "Cordis Emollitio" (softening of the
heart) from *Schola Cordis* should be considered in connection
with the first stanza of "The Weeper." The motto reads
"Deus molluit cor meum." [43] (God has softened my heart.)
The meditation explains that God's grace can melt even
hearts of ice. Anima is blinded by the bright rays proceeding
from Divine Love; the rays reach her frozen heart, which
melts, forming a pool. But an imaginative reader should have
guessed, before reading this description, what a seventeenth-
century emblematist would do with the Biblical metaphor,
"God has softened my heart." He merely represents it graphically, literally, connecting each sensuous particular with a
concept. Crashaw does exactly this. In fact, we are dealing
with a clearly traceable circuit here: from Biblical or proverbial metaphor into graphic representation and then back
again into poetic metaphor. This, to put it briefly, is the
probable history of many of Crashaw's images.

Of course, it is not suggested that Crashaw, typically,
wrote his poems with an emblem book open before him, consciously hunting for useful images. That is, Crashaw is not
always indebted to a *specific* emblematic picture to which we

can readily point. It was the emblematic mode of expression more than individual emblem plates that affected his poetic utterance, although these latter, too, are clearly in evidence. We are concerned, then, with two types of verbal emblem: those which we can trace to specific emblem plates and those for which we are unable, at present, to locate a specific source. One might ask what criteria are applied in labelling an image "emblematic" even when one is unable to suggest a specific source for it. Such an image is termed emblematic when the *pattern* of the emblem is clearly discernible. The image is characterized by a peculiar, often gross, quite unmistakable visual and tactual vividness. There is, furthermore, a dwelling on concrete detail, on sensuous particulars, which are directly related to clear concepts, religious or moralistic. The reader who is acquainted with seventeenth-century emblem literature immediately suspects that such an image has been borrowed from an emblem book, could easily prepare a graphic representation, provide it with a motto, and insert it into, let us say, *Pia Desideria*, where it would appear perfectly at home.

This chapter has concerned itself with analyzing the intellectual element in Crashaw's poetry, but it has not suggested that Crashaw is so intellectually profound or subtle as Donne; indeed, Crashaw's concepts, though clear, are usually theological commonplaces and would hardly have appeared peculiar to his Catholic or Anglican contemporaries. Even less can it be maintained that for Crashaw poetry was an instrument of explication or psychological analysis or exploration. Crashaw, unlike Donne, *accepts* ideas without question. He is concerned not with dialectics, ordinarily, but with meditating on the Christian truths and their significance for believers. And yet the intellectual nature of the imagery needs stressing precisely because most studies ignore it or even explicitly deny it. Even such a sympathetic critic as Mr. E. I. Watkin can classify Crashaw's imagery as richly sensuous and "Keatsian." [44] Actually, it is hard to find a group of poets whose use of imagery differs more essentially from Crashaw's than the early nineteenth-century romanticists. Meditative and objective—these are the epithets which best describe Crashaw's religious lyrics.

NOTES

[1] Mario Praz, *Secentismo e Marinismo in Inghilterra: John Donne e Richard Crashaw* (Florence, 1925), p. 229.

[2] George Williamson, *The Donne Tradition* (New York, 1958), p. 113.

[3] Odette de Mourgues, *Metaphysical, Baroque, and Précieux Poetry* (Oxford, 1953), Ch. III & IV, esp. pp. 83–84.

[4] Robert Adams, "Taste and Bad Taste in Metaphysical Poetry: Richard Crashaw and Dylan Thomas," *The Hudson Review*, VIII (1955), p. 271.

[5] See Eleanor McCann's discussion of food imagery in the writings of Spanish mystics, in *The Influence of Spanish Mystics on Some Seventeenth Century English Poets* (unpublished dissertation, Stanford, 1953), p. 62.

[6] Joan Bennett, *Four Metaphysical Poets* (New York, 1960), p. 120.

[7] Bennett, p. 122.

[8] Quoted by Helen C. White, *The Metaphysical Poets* (New York, 1936), pp. 230–231.

[9] White, p. 231.

[10] A. Alvarez, *The School of Donne* (London, 1961), p. 93.

[11] Michael F. Moloney, "Richard Crashaw," *Catholic World*, CLXII (October, 1945), pp. 43–50. See also "Richard Crashaw" by same author, same periodical, CLXIX (1949), pp. 336–340.

[12] Wylie Sypher, *Four Stages of Renaissance Style* (New York, 1955), p. 187.

[13] Quoted in *Four Stages of Renaissance Style*, p. 185.

[14] Alvarez, p. 99.

[15] Geoffrey Whitney, *A Choice of Emblemes, and other Devises* (Leyden, 1586), p. 57. (Whitney probably borrowed this emblem from Alciati.)

[16] Benedictus van Haeften, *Schola Cordis* (Antwerp, 1629). I am quoting from a German translation, *Hertzen Schuel* (Augsburg, 1664), pp. 656–662 (emblem plate on p. 656). This was one of the most popular emblem books, running through three more editions at Antwerp, translated into English in 1647 with the title *Scola* (sic) *Cordis*. Also worth studying is *Regia Via Crucis* by the same author (Antwerp, 1635).

[17] Francis Quarles, *Emblemes* (London, 1635). I quote from the 1755 edition prepared by William Tegg (London). The emblem in question, p. 378, is entitled "The New Wine of the Heart out of the Press of the Cross" (epigram No. 47). The same emblem appears in *Schola Cordis* p. 646, with the motto "Vinum lactificat cor hominis" and in Daniel Cramer, *Emblematum Sacrorum Prima Pars* (Frankfort, 1624), p. 50.

[18] *Schola Cordis*, p. 602. See pp. 603–605 for meditation. Motto reads "Dabo tibi poculum ex vino conditio. Cant. 8." Quarles reproduces a similar emblem (entitled "The Heart a Cup to a Thirsting Christ"), p. 369, followed by the couplet "Refuse the cup of gall, O spouse divine;/ But wounded hearts afford a pleasant wine." Quarles, however, prepares a meditation quite different from van Haeften's.

[19] *Amoris Divini et Humani Effectus Varii Sacrae Scripturae Sanctorumque* (Antwerp, 1626), p. 29. (This emblem book went through at least five more editions before the end of the century.)

[20] Herman Hugo, *Pia Desideria Emblematis Elegiis & affectibus S. S. Patrum illustrata*. (Antwerp, 1624), pp. 204–205. (Hugo's was perhaps the most popular emblem book on the continent, and even in England before Quarles' publication in 1635.)

[21] Joachim Camerarius (Chambrier), emblem materials published in four volumes:

> *Symbolorum & Emblematum ex re Herbaria desumtorum centuria una* (Nuremberg, 1590).
> *Symbolorum & Emblematum ex Animalibus Quadrupedibus desumtorum centuria altera collecta* (Nuremberg, 1595).
> *Symbolorum & Emblematum ex Volatilibus et Insectis*

desumtorum centuria tertia collecta (Nuremberg, 1596).
Symbolorum et Emblematum ex Aquatilibus et Reptilibus Desumptorum (sic) Centuria Quarta (Nuremberg, 1604).
(These volumes were reprinted more than six times throughout the course of the seventeenth century.)

22 Some especially interesting emblems are Beza's anti-Catholic use of the phoenix (representing Protestant martyrs), Theodore de Beze, *Icones, id est verae imagines virorum doctrina simul et pietate illustrium* (Geneva, 1580), p. 229, Whitney's detailed description of the phoenix's perfumed nest, almost identical to Crashaw's in treatment, p. 177, and Schoonhovius' unusual adaptation of the pelican emblem, Florentius Schoonhovius, *Emblemata Florentii* (sic) (Gouda, 1618), p. 150.

23 Andrew Willet, *Sacrorum Emblematum Centuria Una* (Cambridge, 1592–1598), emblem No. 3 (This work is written in Latin verse, followed by the author's own English translations.) There is no pagination, although the emblem plates are numbered. All citations are from Book III.

24 George Wither, *A Collection of emblemes, ancient and moderne* (London, 1635), Illustr. XXXIX.

25 *Amoris Divini et Humani Effectus*, p. 40.

26 Quarles, pp. 37–39.

27 *Amoris Divini et Humani Effectus*, p. 34.

28 *Amoris Divini et Humani Effectus*, p. 13. See also pp. 14, 19.

29 *Ibid.*, p. 24.

30 Quarles, pp. 279–330.

31 Quarles, p. 223.

32 Wither, pp. 102–140, 159, 209. See also Hugo, pp. 302–304.

33 Wither, p. 178.

34 Vaenius, *Amorum Emblemata*, pp. 188–189.

35 Vaenius, *Amoris Divini Emblemata*, p. 18.

36 Wither, p. 91.

37 Beza, No. XIX ("Annulus pretiosa gemma ornatus"). (Pagination is often obscured.)

38 Hugo, p. 58.

39 Hugo, pp. 304–305.

40 *Amoris Divini et Humani Effectus*, p. 21.

41 Vaenius, *Amoris Divini Emblemata*, p. 23.

[42] Hugo, pp. 368–369. Quarles' copy (p. 220) is artistically unsatisfactory, for it is unable to reproduce the facial expressions with sufficient detail.

[43] *Schola Cordis*, p. 253.

[44] E. I. Watkin, *Poets and Mystics* (London, 1953), p. 158.

THE INFLUENCE OF
ST. FRANCIS DE SALES

*Crashaw in Relation to the Devotional Climate
of Seventeenth Century England*

Professor Helen C. White has reminded us that in the religious life of the seventeenth century nothing happens in a
water-tight compartment.[1] Perhaps no Protestant country
during our period felt the influence of contemporary continental Catholicism so strongly as did England, thanks partly
to the Douay Press. Continental devotional books, both the
originals and their translations, Professor White assures us,
had great vogue in seventeenth-century England.[2] Elizabethan law sentenced Robert Southwell to a horrible death
but evidently did not object to the publication, in 1591, of
his prose meditation "Marie Magdalen's Funeral Tears." Giles
Randall translated the third part of *La Règle de Perfection,* a
mystical treatise published a few years earlier by the Capu-
chin convert Benet Canfield. Peter Sterry, leader of the In-
dependents, driven from his pulpit by the Restoration, ac-
knowledges his debt to the example of holiness set by the

Catholic de Renty, an "example fixed with much dearness and esteem upon my heart." [3] And in a sermon preached to the house of Commons, in which he compares Romans to Presbyterians, he admits that Catholics take and give "large scope to the understanding and affections in generous contemplation." [4] Even the fiercely anti-Papal William Crashaw (father of Richard Crashaw), who warns the members of the Virginia Company not to suffer Popery in the colonies, complains that the Papists have surely outdone the Protestants in the composing of edifying books of devotion, so much so that it is sometimes necessary to have recourse to these books, which, were it not for their occasional superstitious passages, would be highly commendable. [5]

Especially interesting is the attitude of the Puritan Baxter concerning Catholic devotional works. In *Christian Ecclesiastics* he considers the problem of Protestants consorting with Roman Catholics. Quite unequivocally he outlaws participation at mass and "other such abominable idolatries" but assures his readers that they may with good conscience read the many sound devotional books and meditation manuals composed by contemporary Papists. [6] He extends the same liberality to Catholic (even Jesuit) theological treatises on noncontroversial matters. Thus we find that among the theological treatises which Baxter recommends to students affluent enough to afford a private library are a treatise by Suarez and one by Bellarmine, both Jesuits. [7]

Nor was the use of Catholic hymns an unheard of practice. William Crashaw translated a good number of these, and the open publication of undisguisedly Catholic poems (usually paraphrases of Catholic hymns, it would seem) reaches its heights during the Puritan regime, especially during the years 1646 and 1648. If even the Puritans, whose dislike of Catholicism was so whole-hearted, permitted themselves such a degree of intimate companionship with Catholic authors, one should not be surprised to learn that Catholic reading was common at Peterhouse. And if the disciples of Baxter were permitted to read certain Catholic devotional books, surely one should expect to find the same books in the hands of Laud's disciples. If a student wishes to assess the various currents of thought which exerted their influences on Richard Crashaw, he must, above all else, be keenly aware of this openness in the intellectual climate of the day, especially in matters of devotion and meditation. The study of currents of religious influence in Renaissance England and attempts to classify devotional writers of this period have often suffered from procedures based upon an assumption that Counter-Reformation Catholicism and Protestantism (at least Puritanism) were indeed two water-tight compartments. Two separate compartments they were; but with perforated walls. This study of the influence of St. Francis de Sales requires the reader to keep continually in mind the nature of the intellectual and religious milieu. Because the openness of that atmosphere is not often acknowledged, a convenient dichotomization being typical of most studies, it seems advisable to expand this study of certain aspects of seventeenth-century Protestant spirituality.

The religious sensibility known as the Baroque is too often regarded as a phenomenon peculiar to Counter-Reformation Catholicism. More accurately, Counter-Reformation sensibility is one of several manifestations of a much broader religious spirit—the Baroque. *Baroque*, as applied to spirituality, will be a much more functional term if we remember that the qualities which we ascribe to it characterize seventeenth-century religion *in general*. Much of what some scholars, including Austin Warren, have attributed to direct continental influence was simply "in the air" often in widely separated countries, a phenomenon usually due to parallel sociological and intellectual movements. Of course, a spiral effect is involved here. The very fact that a certain attitude is already more or less "in the air" in early seventeenth-century England renders readers especially receptive to eloquent expositions or developments of that point of view. To speak imagistically, these common attitudes are the perforations which permitted so much gushing between the two compartments. It will be advisable, then, to reexamine briefly the religious climate of early seventeenth-century England, not to highlight the differences between the Catholic and Protestant spirits, but to demonstrate certain important points of unity.

It would be hard to find a topic more furiously debated between Catholics and Protestants of the early seventeenth century than the use of religious images. Judging from the copious Puritan polemics, one concludes that the iconoclastic fury of Geneva had not yet spent itself. Meanwhile Latin Catholicism was simultaneously enriching and laying increased emphasis on the iconic element in devotion, for it was the policy of the Council of Trent to single out for special stress those very dogmas and religious practices which the Protestants had rejected. The spirit of Counter-Reformation Catholicism is that of an aggressive, high spirited army, wary of its enemy but anticipating glory. Nevertheless, it is a mistake to attribute the expansive, energetic overstatement typical of both Baroque art and poetry, and the brilliant imagistic effects, solely to this Catholic militancy, for there are too many Protestant counterparts to the specifically Roman Catholic Baroque, counterparts so conspicuous that one marvels to find them almost always overlooked.

Even among the Puritans of the period one is struck by an expansiveness and energy of spirit close enough to that of Latin Catholicism to mark it as a different manifestation of a general sensibility. And among the Puritans, too, there is ample evidence of the Baroque eagerness to embody spiritual truths in icons, although unlike their Laudian brothers, they had to confine their icon-making to the verbal and mental spheres, to literature and to mental prayer.

For this tendency to image religious thought and feeling one can offer at least two explanations, one of which has already been suggested—the general crisis in faith and conscience. In England the most worldly aspects of the Renaissance were at their height during the first few decades of the seventeenth century, and the "new philosophy" was making more headway there than it was in many places. The guarantee of the senses was perhaps highly welcome.

But there is another explanation, one directly related to what I believe to be the central tendency of religious life in Renaissance Europe—the increasing emphasis on personal, meditative prayer. This emphasis on mental prayer is simply the culmination of a slowly growing movement with roots in the early middle ages. The increasing tendencies toward introspection and individuality did much to encourage this meditative tradition, especially that developed by St. Ignatius de Loyola. But at the same time, the trying tensions of the age, generated in part by hectic religious controversy, in part by the "new philosophy" and in part by the literary and geographical recoveries and discoveries of the Renaissance, drove many people to private, meditative devotion of a type which, as Baxter promised, would unite all the powers of the soul.

Whatever the causes of this phenomenon, of this much we can be certain: in the words of Louis Martz, the "meditative methods of the Continent became embedded in English life and literature of the seventeenth century." [8] That meditation is essential to leading the Christ-life "is allowed by all," the Puritan Baxter tells us. [9] This meditative piety, by its very nature, encouraged, perhaps even demanded, a highly imagistic type of thinking and feeling.

The student of the literature of the period must remind himself that the minds of those men who rushed with axe and torch to destroy the religious pictures of Peterhouse were quite likely veritable galleries of rich, sensuous icons, eager to be pressed into the service of fervent meditation. Despoil chapels of their icons they might, but they created new ones in their own imaginations; for to this mental icon-making almost everything in the Puritan tradition conduced. And as one reads the numerous Puritan diatribes against the "idolatry" of the Papists, he can hardly avoid being struck by the fascination of these Puritans with the icons. Fear them, abominate them they may, but in the spirit that one despises a beautiful, almost irresistibly alluring evil. They understand quite well, suspiciously well, the temptation to terminate devotion at the level of the icon. But they made their own contributions to iconology.

Thus, it is quite wrong to assume that Crashaw wrote or read in an atmosphere in which any significant portion of population (including his own father as we shall soon see) objected to even the lavish use of icons in either mental prayer or religious poetry. It is in his subject matter occasionally, in attitude often, but surely not in *poetic method* that Richard Crashaw runs counter to the Puritan tradition.

His Papist-hating father, William Crashaw, translated an extremely florid poem by a Flemish Jesuit Bonarsch, who expresses the desire spiritually to suck our Lady's milk and the blood flowing from Christ's wounds. Now, William Crashaw attacks the author for allegedly maintaining that the milk of the Virgin is more excellent than the blood of Christ; but, significantly, he picks no quarrel with the poetic method or the nature of the symbolism. Indeed, his careful retouching of the poem, as Watkin suggests, is an indication of his appreciation for the poetry and taste.

The Puritans themselves were capable of florid, fiery religious writing. Especially noteworthy is that fascinating man, Francis Rous, a bitter opponent of the Laudian movement, more Calvinistic than Baxter. One of his works is a highly important parallel to the poems of Crashaw, precisely because of the rabid Puritanism of the author. In 1635 Rous published his "Mysticall Marriage or Experimental Discourses of the Heavenly Marriage between a Soul and her Savior." [10] According to Rous the best way to consider the relationship between the soul and Christ her Savior is that provided by the Holy Spirit Himself in the *Song of Songs,* for "There is a chamber within us, and a bed of love within that chamber wherein Christ meetes and rests with the soule." The spiritual life is discussed in great detail as a divine romance during which the "Soule seeketh her husband and finds Him," and after a generous sprinkling of Neoplatonic elements and several theological complexities, Rous concludes that "as man and wife in a corporeal marriage are one flesh, so in this spiritual and mysticall marriage, Christ and his spouse become one spirit." Christ so loves all souls that he will make them his "wives"; the "spirit of Christ enters and lays in them an immortal seed" and "by his precious blood purgeth her from guilt."

The soul must look upon Christ and Christ alone as the "true object of her inflamed affection," for as "the body lusteth after what is carnal, so the spirit lusteth after Christ, her husband." The devout believer should address Christ in the following way, after picturing him visibly present and gazing lovingly upon Him: "Yea, kisse my soule with such a kisse of thy spirit that they may be no longer two, but one spirit; my soule thirsteth and panteth for thee." Rous also urges, "Tell him thou art sicke of love for Him; winde thy affections round about him."

Before continuing I wish to remind the reader that this author is no rejected maverick; he became Speaker of the Barebones Parliament and a leading Cromwellian peer. Much of this devotional tract consists of complicated analogies, such as the one comparing the sinful soul to an adulterous woman, concluding that the coupling of a soul and lust is like the intercourse of a woman and a hideous beast. Then Rous develops another analogy: the soul that would be united to Christ must become widowed; the first husband, earthly and carnal, must die. But betrothal, he tells us, is a better work than marriage, for the consummation of this spiritual marriage takes place in heaven. Even this betrothal, though, is so rapturous as to "cast darkness on all the joy in the world."

This Puritan zealot, once Provost of Eton, is capable of passages such as these, which should interest the student of Crashaw:

> The dew of his birth is of the wombe of the morning, even of that morning which hath an everlasting rising. (p. 48)

> Oh the utmost sweetness of the taste of God . . . an ecstasy and ravishment, a joy too great for the weak spirit. (p. 48)

> . . . the heavenly wine sucked from the prime and chiefest spirit, how doth that ravish the spirits that drinke it . . . (p. 48)

> . . . tho the flesh Enlarge the crany which thy spirit hath bored into my spirit, that I may see thee . . . Enlarge the arteries and conduit pipes, by which thou the head and fountaine of love, flowest into thy members, that being abundantly quickened and watered with the spirit of love I may abundantly love thee . . . . . . Hony and Sweetnesse itselfe to the soule that loveth her beloved comes quickly. (p. 342)

Rous concludes his devotional tract with an impassioned prayer, the following section of which is worth serious attention:

> O thou fountaine and rest of loves: thy ointments draw her (my soul) to the anoynter, her loves begin and end in thee. O let my soule ever runne the circle of loves; let her ever be tasting of thy loves and ever love thee by tasting them. Let the savour of thy oyntments, whose very breath is love, be ever in her nostrils, that she may ever love thee of that savour, and by it. Give me flagons of the new wine of thy kingdome, which may lift up my soule above herselfe in her loves, and give her better than her owne . . . Yea, let her drink plentifully that she may be mounted up in divine extasie above her carnall and earthly station; that she may forget the low and base griefes and cares and distractions of carnall and worldly love, and by an heavenly excesse be transported from heaven, with a love that is like him . . . O my beloved, thou are most lovely. But then thy lovelinesse is lost to me, because love loves not what it sees not. Therefore ever anoynt mine eyes with thine eye-salve. (p. 379)

Henceforth, let us be wary, all of us, of the term *anima naturaliter Catholica*, the epithet which Mario Praz has applied to Crashaw, to set him apart from his countrymen.

Mystical fervor, Baroque sensuousness—both are as abundant here as anywhere in Crashaw, and in Rous too we are struck by the profusion of ravishing ointments, sweet-tasting substances, and "sweet inebriated ecstasies." No Italian or French devotional tract which I have read surpasses Rous' in Baroque exuberance or in bold appropriation of the sexual imagery of the *Song of Songs*. It is hard to generalize about the English Puritans, and no attempt has been made here to lump all of them together. But what is insisted on is that a fiery exuberance and even a lusciousness of imagery amazingly akin to that of Counter-Reformation Catholicism are not infrequently encountered among some segments of English Protestants. And it seems safe enough to suggest that the farther left we move from center, the more likely we are to encounter this fervent religion.

Symbolic imagery is not the only point of similarity between seventeenth-century Puritanism and continental Catholicism. These two different manifestations of the Christian spirit have more in common than has been realized, even if we consider devotional emphasis alone. Tender, deep devotion to Jesus, for instance, is a characteristic of much Puritan religion. Especially illuminating is Professor Watkin's study of a work of Thomas Godwin (Chaplain to Cromwell), "The Heart of Christ in Heaven towards Sinners on Earth, or a Treatise demonstrating the Gracious disposition and tender affection of Christ in his Human nature." Strangely enough, it seems to be an anticipation of the Catholic devotion to the Sacred Heart of Jesus. This favorite preacher of the Long Parliament assures us that whatever we cannot understand in the nature of things is a glorious mystery of Divine Love. Godwin's purpose is to lay open "the heart of Christ, as now He is in heaven to show how it is affected and graciously disposed towards sinners on earth that do come to Him, how willing to receive them, His heart in respect of pity and compassion, remains the same as it was on earth. . . ." [11]

At this point many readers will have concluded that a really definitive study of the Puritan religious heritage remains to be written. There are few subjects about which literary critics toss out inaccurate cliches more glibly than English Puritanism. But this partial view of Puritanism implicit or explicit in most studies has appreciably affected verdicts on the poetry of Crashaw. Those to whom he appears, at worst, foreign-hearted and alien and, at best, a member of a small group of Anglo-Catholics quite unrepresentative of the religious temper of seventeenth-century England, will rid themselves of this erroneous but almost universal impression only by steeping themselves in the devotional literature of the time, both English and continental, Protestant and Catholic. They will do well, also, to remember that Cowley apologized for Crashaw's conversion to Roman Catholicism but *not* for his subject matter, much less for his poetic method. No, it is the neo-classical stomach, not the Puritan one, which finds Crashaw indigestible.

This glance at certain aspects of the religious climate of early seventeenth-century England, especially after the first two decades, has seemed necessary to enable the student of Crashaw to view the formation of his mind and of his poetic method in a new perspective. Students of English literature have never found it easy to place Crashaw in the mainstream of English poetry. This difficulty arises largely from lack of awareness that many Englishmen of those times were in fact steeped in what we now regard as foreign and Latin elements. Like all literary manifestations, the Baroque existed on a spectrum. It is interesting that those manifestations of the Baroque which to many of us appear grossly sensuous occur far more frequently in prose and poetry of second and especially third rate merit than in those works of the aristocratic tradition with which critics are far more familiar. It is easy to forget, after all, that the poets who have understandably received the lion's share of critical attention are not necessarily those most widely read by the seventeenth-century public. It seems certain, for instance, that at least ten Englishmen read and enjoyed the enormously popular, often third rate verse of Quarles for every one who read *Comus* or even the *Steps to the Temple*. And Quarles abounds in just those manifestations of the Baroque which have alienated many moderns from Crashaw.

Neither space nor the scope of this book permits the expansion or generous demonstration of the point about to be made (although I have set this task for myself in a future work). Seventeenth-century criticism has had surprisingly little to do with second and third rate writers. This emphasis on authors in the main tradition, although completely justifiable, has yielded an inaccurate picture of popular sensibility. Much of the devotional poetry of the time—Quarles' to name the most popular—and many of the sermons of the period—to name the most widely read genre—can be described only as hack writing, but no scholar who wishes to describe popular sensibility or culture can ignore it. Whoever sets for himself the not always appealing task of delving into this third rate literature (so difficult to obtain, at present) is startled by the abundance of sensuous, even gross, Baroque elements. And the farther he strays from the main tradition, the more often does he encounter these manifestations, and the grosser they become. One is tempted to suggest that there existed a Baroque "pop culture," quite apart from the aristocratic tradition, a popular culture at its height in the third and fourth decades of the century, destined to disappear rapidly after the Restoration.

It seems, then, that Crashaw's debt was not exclusively to Marino and the European Baroque poets. He had recourse, as well, perhaps much more extensively, to a native tradition largely eschewed by his contemporaries in the aristocratic tradition. This latter tradition toned down, moderated the most sensuous aspects of the Baroque, which were manifested much more openly in popular literature.

We have asserted that Englishmen of the early seventeenth century were steeped in what we today call "foreign and Latin" elements. But it is difficult to determine, in many cases, whether a given manifestation of the Baroque is a native development of some aspect of the continuing medieval tradition which survived the Reformation, or whether it is an adaptation of a continental importation. It is worth pointing out, also, that continental Baroque borrowings were not always Catholic in origin. It would be interesting, for example, to study the influence of the Genevan emblem books (one of which was composed by Theodore Bèze himself), a remarkable example of the Puritan Baroque.

And anyone widely acquainted with emblem literature smiles at the traditional equation of Latin or Italian with "sensuous" religion. Actually, it is the Northern emblematists, the Dutch and the Germans especially, who developed the sensuous, erotic elements of the Baroque to their highest peak. Divine Love, disguised as Cupid, armed with heart-piercing arrows and jars of irresistible perfumes, was received far more cordially in the homeland of Erasmus than in the land of Dante, a region which, incidentally, He did not much frequent. And I know of no passage in Marino which approaches the grossness of, let us say, Quarles' Epigram No. 47. In a word, we have missed the English Baroque.

But even if many of the ingredients that went to form the final product which we call the Crashaw religious outlook were of native origin, the all important matter of proportion, of emphasis and deemphasis, was influenced to a great extent by the works of St. Francis de Sales. This influence was possible because the Bishop of Geneva struck in Crashaw a chord irresistibly soothing and enchanting; for our poet as for so many in those times, the saintly Savoyard provided needed balm for the unbearable strain which the religious life of the times was inflicting on sensitive souls.

Surely readers who could digest Rous' metaphors or even Sterry's and Godwin's would have found nothing unpalatable in the works of St. Francis de Sales; that is, not from the viewpoint of style or temper. Both in translation and in the original language, his works had great vogue in seventeenth-century England. His *Introduction to a Devout Life* was translated into English and published at Douai in 1613; in 1614 there appeared a new English edition (that of Yakesley). From this date on, the *Introduction* was the most popular of Catholic books anywhere. Marie de Medici had a copy of it sent bound in gold and gems to James I.[12]

Almost as influential in England was St. Francis' *Traité de l'Amour de Dieu,* translated into English in 1630 by Crashaw's friend, Thomas Carre (whose real name was Miles Pinkney), by which time eighteen French editions had already appeared. Crashaw's father, who maintained a library of "Popish" books for refutation, must surely have possessed copies of these two extremely popular and influential books. It is possible that Crashaw was exposed to St. Francis even before his Cambridge days.

It was Anthony F. Allison who first pointed out the influence of St. Francis de Sales. After stating that Crashaw could hardly have failed to read him at Cambridge, Allison proposes several direct borrowings, which will be summarized here.[13] Quite striking, for instance, is the concluding couplet found in both editions of *Steps to the Temple:* "Live Jesus, Live, and let it bee/My life to dye, for love of thee." This couplet seems inspired by the concluding chapter of the *Traité,* Book XII, Chapter 13: "To love or to die! To die and to love! To die to all other love in order to live to Jesus, who lives and reigns for ever and ever." Also attributable to St. Francis is the maxim that to be eloquent one need only love, found in lines 7–10 of the "Apologie for the Foregoing Hymn." And in "The Flaming Heart" Crashaw's development of the wound of love metaphor suggests not St. Teresa but St. Francis, who adds considerably to her account of the wound of love.

Allison is quite right in insisting that Crashaw's language

suggests that he had read and remembered de Sales' detailed analysis of the reciprocal nature of the wound and its relationship to Christ's sacrifice on Calvary.[14] In "An Apologie for the Foregoing Hymn" (lines 34–37) Crashaw urges his soul to drink until it becomes an angel, contrasting it to those men who drink until they become beasts. This concept, of the two sorts of extravagance of which man is capable, one from human weakness and the other from divine rapture, is a familiar feature of Neoplatonic thought and received particular emphasis in the syncretistic writings attributed to Mercurius Trismegistus. It was revived in the fifteenth century by Ficino of the Platonic Academy. But surely it is more probable, as Allison maintains, that this theme of dual ecstasy was borrowed from the *Traité*.

But there is another borrowing which in my opinion is more striking than any of those which Allison has proposed. The following (translated) quotation from the *Traité* deserves close study in connection with "The Weeper":

(English translation)

As far as I know, nature has never turned fire into water, although water has been turned into fire on many occasions. But God did so once as a miracle (that is, turned fire into water) . . . .

Theotime, amid the tribulations and remorse of a lively repentance, God often enkindles at the bottom of our hearts the sacred fire of His love; then this love turns itself into the water of copious tears, which, through a second change, are turned into another, and greater, fire of love. Thus that illustrious lover (of Christ, Mary Magdalene) first loved our savior when she repented; this love turned into sobs, and these sobs into a more excellent love. Thus our Lord said that many sins were forgiven her, because she had loved much . . . .

Look, I ask of you, Theotime, at the well-beloved Magdalene, how she weeps out of love . . . .

Remorse for sin produces the water of holy repentance; then from this water there comes, in reciprocal fashion, the fire of divine love, which can be called, quite properly, water of life and *burning water* (italics mine). It is certainly, in substance, water; for repentance is nothing but a sincere dislike, a truly painful remorse. But it (repentance) is burning also because it contains the power and the characteristics of love, proceeding as it does from motives of divine love. And because of this characteristic (of love) it confers the life of supernatural grace. This is why perfect contrition has two different effects: in virtue of the pain and loathing of sin which it involves, it has bound us (attaché) but in virtue of the motive of divine love, it reunites us to God, from whom we were cut off because of our sins.[15]

Now let us read what is obviously Crashaw's terse, emblematic rendition, in "The Weeper" (1652 edition):

XVII

O sweet content! of woes
with loves; of teares with smiles disputing!
O fair and friendly foes,
Each other kissing and confuting!
While rain and sunshine, cheekes and eyes
Close in kind contrarietyes

XVIII

But can these fair flouds be
Friends with the bosom—fires that till thee!
Can so great flames agree
Aeternal teares should thus distill thee!
O flouds! O fires! O suns! O showres!
Mixt and made friends by Louve's sweet powres.

Also worthy of note is the couplet appearing directly under the title in the 1648 edition but consigned to the engraving in "Carmen Deo Nostro": "Is she a flaming fountain, or a weeping fire?"

But direct borrowings are by no means the most significant influence of St. Francis de Sales on Crashaw. While it is true that the great majority of those attitudes and doctrines that make up Crashaw's religious outlook were part of the religious atmosphere surrounding him (if not always dominant in it, at least not alien to it), St. Francis de Sales, as was stated before, seems to have played the major role in the actual selection of ingredients and in the determining of the degree of emphasis each element was to receive. The Salesian spirit shines almost everywhere in Crashaw; and this spirit, one should recall, was in part a reaction to certain dominant religious attitudes and emphases of the late sixteenth and early seventeenth centuries.

Few religious writers have spoken so directly and eloquently to their age as St. Francis de Sales did. It is almost as if he had examined the religious spirit of his day, diagnosed its ailments, and then set himself to writing a series of prescriptions in beautiful prose. If early seventeenth-century religious man needed to be reminded of anything, it was of God's ineffable love for mankind. The judgment of God, the flames of hell, the miseries of human life have perhaps never been more dramatically stressed. And the Predestinarian view, which had once been a source of comfort, gave signs of producing great strain on the seventeenth-century religious man. An unquestioning faith in God's overwhelming love for His creation, a love utterly surpassing man's understanding, is the cornerstone of Salesian doctrine. Even more than that, it is an introductory chord which establishes the tonality of every line St. Francis de Sales wrote; and from this key there is not modulation. Even sin, death, and damnation are not for one moment viewed apart from this one central belief. Reviewing New Testament figures to whom one might compare the Bishop of Geneva, we can consider only one—St. John the beloved Apostle.

So it should not surprise us that the very first meditation which St. Francis recommends to his spiritual daughter Philothea is God's love for all the world in general and for her in particular. Not until she is thoroughly convinced of God's burning love for her can she hope to make progress in the spiritual life. She is urged to reflect on the numerous benefits and kindnesses which she should see bestowed everywhere around her.[16]

In the *Traité* St. Francis studies the question of God's love for man in greater detail than any theologian had previously done. It is God's love which sustains every creature in being, and so ardently does Heaven desire the redemption of men that the angels rejoice more exuberantly over the conversion of the worst sinners than over the security of those already saved. It is love and love alone which impels every act of God. And de Sales is fond of describing this charity emblematically, as the sun which warms, beautifies, and vivifies all.

The spiritual life, too, is seen entirely in terms of love. To progress spiritually is, by definition, to love God increasingly. The conversion from sin to grace is described as streaks of dawn dispelling the darkest night; as the penitent grows toward perfection, the light of the Sun, which is God's love, grows stronger, whiter, clearer. But except for miraculous cases (such as Mary Magdalene's) darkness is expelled slowly.

The last rule in Loyola's *Spiritual Exercises* asserts that it is praiseworthy to serve God out of pure love, but that we ought to prize the fear of God too and not only filial fear but even servile fear. But St. Francis, while he recognizes that fear might be the motive which first impels the sinner toward God, insists that little spiritual progress is made until this fear is entirely converted to love. Love, not fear of God's wrath, is what must prompt all human actions. In a letter to his favorite disciple, St. Jane de Chantal, he proposes the following motto as the chief rule for her life, in bold capital letters:

LOVE AND NOT FORCE SHOULD INSPIRE ALL
YOU DO:
LOVE OBEDIENCE MORE THAN YOU FEAR
DISOBEDIENCE.[17]

Every act motivated by charity ascends to God with a sweet savor.[18] And although a certain degree of knowledge is necessary before one can love God, this love itself becomes a source of knowledge, by divine infusion. Thus St. Catherine of Genoa, although an "idote femme," knew more about Christ than such a scholar as William of Occam.

The loss of God's grace is what St. Francis always stresses in describing the effects of serious sin. His meditations on Hell pass over the flames and brimstone with a rapidity and lightness certain to startle a reader versed in Renaissance devotional works. "Can you endure parting with your God forever?" This everlasting estrangement is what he stresses, never the physical torments of Hell.

And only in one context does St. Francis dwell on the wrath of God. The sin of ingratitude is the one matter which this ordinarily serene Bishop cannot discuss without betraying anger. This sin, which he treats in detail, is a hideous blight which "extends itself over all the other sins one might commit, making them infinitely more enormous." It is the sin which man should most fear, for God is angry at seeing His priceless gifts ignored and despised. Curiously, St. Francis speaks of God's wrath only in this context.

We should not be surprised, then, to find that in Crashaw's

world, too, the love of God is everywhere manifest. Arno Esch, speaking of the subject matter of Crashaw's poems, states that "Sein Hauptthema ist das Mysterium der göttlichen Liebe," [19] but perhaps it is more accurate to say that Crashaw's favorite subject matter is *Christ's* love for man and the love of the saints for him. Crashaw, so much more than St. Francis, specifies the person of Christ as the Divine Lover. But divine love, certainly, is Crashaw's main theme, as he announces in his introductory poem "Lectori" (To the Reader):

> Scilicet ille tuos ignis recalescet ad ignes;
> Forsan et illa tuis unda natabit aquis
> His eris ad cunas, et odoros funere manes:
> Hinc ignes nasci testis, et inde meos.[20]

Crashaw sees in everything a sign of Christ's love. Tears are always beautiful and precious because they are a sign of the penitent's love and thus, in a way, a guarantee of his redemption. They are pleasing, also, to the divine Lover, since they are a sign of love for him. And the very fact that they flow at all is proof of Christ's love for the repentant sinner, since the first step in conversion from sin to grace requires the assistance of heavenly grace. In the Crucifixion also, the wounds and blood of Christ are usually symbols of love, beautiful and precious not only because they are Christ's, but also because they heal mankind spiritually. St. Francis de Sales urges his readers to meditate often on the Crucifixion to become increasingly aware of God's overwhelming love for men and to feel pity for the Divine Victim, thus growing in divine love.

Only three of Crashaw's sacred epigrams have the Crucifixion as their subject. What is particularly striking about all three is the curiously unreal quality of the imagery. (As we shall see later, the Salesian meditative method is largely responsible for this.) There is no attempt on the poet's part to recreate the horror of that moment; indeed, the poetic technique would militate against such an aim, for no sooner are wounds and blood mentioned than they become symbols to be juggled rhetorically. What the poet does emphasize in all three Crucifixion poems is the preciousness of the Saving Blood and its marvelous effect on mankind. The horrible extent of Christ's suffering is a minor theme at the most, as with St. Francis.

Not only in the Crucifixion, but in almost every Biblical event, Crashaw, like his spiritual master, manages to find evidence of Christ's love. In "Our Blessed Lord in His Circumcision to His Father," God views the Circumcision smilingly, for this first shedding of His Son's blood is an act of love. Blood, with Crashaw, is invariably a symbol of love manifested through suffering. And it is highly characteristic of Crashaw that martyrdom, a theme which he celebrates several times, never becomes an occasion for a diatribe against the enemies of Christ, nor even for sorrow. Without exception, martyrdom represents the triumph of resplendent love, both the martyr's and Christ's. Particularly striking is *EIS TON TOY STEΘANOY STEΘANON* (On the Crown of Stephen). In this epigram the stones immediately turn into sparkling diamonds as they touch the head of the martyr, joyfully massing together to form a crown for Stephen, so overcome are they by his immense love for Christ. Very few men except St. Francis de Sales and Crashaw could have viewed martyrdom so serenely.

Even the Magdalen and St. Teresa die for love: their weak bodily frames could not contain a spirit which yearned so ardently to be united to the Beloved. It is for the fullness of their love, above all, that these two women are praised.

Only in a few poems does Crashaw discuss charity explicitly, in a theological manner. One of the most interesting is the Latin poem "Fides, quae sola justificat," a work standing midway between the usual Baroque lyric and neo-classical ratiocinative verse. The poem is also one of the few devoted to matters of dogmatic controversy, with which it deals in an essentially expository manner. One would not wish to grade Crashaw as a theologian or logician on its basis, though. What is interesting is his attempt to reconcile contradictory views. He maintains throughout, or tries to maintain, the traditional Protestant view concerning justification by faith alone: faith and only faith saves, but "saving faith" is then redefined as that which includes hope, charity, good works (a frequent Catholic explanation). Semantic tricks take the place of logic.

In "Upon Five Pious and Learned Discourses" he cries out for a more visible manifestation of charity in the English Church. He wonders whether the Pope is really antichrist. In any case, he is sure it is "no point of charitee." What is needed is less controversy, less preaching, but much more practicing of Christian charity; only in such a way can the English "redeem virtue to action." St. Francis de Sales, too, is almost unique in the mild, gentle tone with which he speaks of his Calvinist adversaries. Rancor is totally missing from his pages.

St. Francis laid great stress on man's inability to love God above his creatures without divine grace. Those first groping movements toward God are manifestations of the grace of Christ working within us, a divine presence. In at least one poem this dogma seems to have inspired Crashaw. The divine epigram "In mulierem Canaanaeam cum Domino decertantem" plays on the conceit that although Christ seems to have yielded to the woman, He is really yielding not to any human power but rather to His own power (grace) within her ("Atque in te vires sentit, amatque suas").

The reader will recall the Bishop of Geneva's condemnations of ingratitude against God. This is one of the few human weaknesses, perhaps the only one if we judge from his poetry, which Crashaw could not view with Salesian detachment. The ingratitude of the cured lepers, for instance, gnawed at him painfully enough to deserve being reproved in three different epigrams. In one of these ("Leprosi Ingrati") the wretches seem implicitly damned, a fate which Crashaw does not lightly dole out to his fellow men:

> Et lepra, quae fuerat corpore, mente sedet.
> Sic igitur digna vice res variatur; et a se
> Quam procul ante homines, nunc habuere Deum.[21]

That God punishes those who trample on his choicest graces by withholding them in the future is a favorite Salesian idea, used in a particularly interesting manner in "On a Prayer Booke."

But perhaps the greatest testimony to the extent of Crashaw's absorption of this Salesian emphasis on the love of God is the very subject matter of the divine epigrams. Better than half of these deal with the miracles wrought by Christ on earth, those involving the healing of the physically afflicted being especially numerous. These miracles are interpreted, usually, as touching testimonies of Christ's love for mankind.

"You will make progress (in the spiritual life) in proportion to the violence you do to yourself." Echoes of this Ignatian maxim resound in most of the devotional books of the times, but nothing could be more alien to Salesian spirituality than this anthropomorphic piety. The Savoyard Bishop insisted on nothing so firmly as on tranquility of soul. True devotion as distinguished from false devotion (rampant in the early seventeenth century according to St. Francis), is prudent, sane, cheerful, never unpleasant, never superstitious, fantastical, or incompatible with the duties of one's state in life. Next to sin the worst evil is "all inquietude." One should beware also of any ruling passion. Even the least inclination to sadness is to be opposed. One should take a stroll with a pleasant companion, give oneself over to licit but joyous activities, or sing spiritual canticles to preserve a constant state of cheerfulness. Another way of curing spells of sadness is speaking to God in words of tender confidence: "My beloved is mine and I am his. My beloved is to me a posy of myrrh, he shall dwell between my breasts. My eyes have fainted after thee, o my God." Of course, one should be diligent in all he does, especially in matters highly relevant to salvation, but even in these things one must never "be agitated by any anxiety at all," but "must maintain a calm and tranquil state of mind." Those who are anxious and worried are like drones, who make wax only, never honey. To torture oneself violently, to afflict oneself with reproaches, is of little value. One should not worry even about spiritual dryness. An attitude of calm suavity should characterize the devout soul at all times, for this tranquility is based not upon complacency or self-satisfaction but upon a deep trust in the goodness of God.

St. Francis has little to say about either Hell or death, and what he does say seems tame stuff indeed to anyone widely read in devotional works of the time. Neither is a favorite subject for meditation:

> But, my daughter, these four meditations on the Four Last Things must all end with hope, not with fear and terror; for when they end with fear especially of death and hell, they are dangerous.[22]

Such is not the usual seventeenth-century way. Again and again he insists that his spiritual daughters are not to torment themselves.

St. Francis proposes what, with many qualifications, may be termed a let-God-do-the-work program for spiritual advancement. No approach has been more theocentric than his. Never does he encourage cultivation of the spiritual self but demands, rather, that it be lost in God. Examination of conscience lies at the very heart of the Ignatian program for spiritual advancement, and from this exercise Ignatius never dispensed. St. Francis, on the other hand, regarded the examination of conscience as less central. He recommends only a short one, at night, during which one is to consider his lapses, ask pardon for them, resolve to confess them, but then proceed directly to consign himself to God's care and to implore divine protection for family and friends. One must combat any scruples or moods of depression which might arise during this time. The intense self-scrutiny of the Spanish mystics, which they had in common with both the Puritans and the followers of Loyola, is precisely what St. Francis quite consciously rejects. Consciously, I say, for although he knew the Ignatian method well, he never once introduces it or recommends it; and he never tires of warning his spiritual charges against autocentric devotions. We should, indeed, consider wherein we have failed, but we must "consider these faults gently," and we ought never "dwell on them long" even when preparing for Confession. Not once does the Bishop of Geneva warn his charges about the dangerous effects of scanty self-knowledge, but frequently tries to lead them away from excessive introspection:

> Peace is lost when self-examination is pushed too far. . . . Let us resign ourselves not to know what we are or where we are. Put away all morbid curiosity, at once cruel and useless; oh stop all indefinite returning to past actions, motives . . . Oh, my dear daughter, avoid all these reflections, for it is impossible for the Spirit of God to dwell in a soul eager to know all that is happening in her! [23]

"It is impossible for the Spirit of God to dwell in a soul eager to know all that is happening in her!" No one ever spoke more directly to early seventeenth-century religious man (or to twentieth-century man?). Here is a spiritual approach which does not encourage a man to take himself too seriously.

But suppose one is guilty of serious sin? To what extent should the attitude of suavity be maintained? Even if we must, St. Francis tells us, arouse our soul to confusion for a few brief moments, we should immediately afterwards close up this grief and anger with a sweet, consoling confidence in God. Then we ask for God's pardon, which he swiftly, eagerly grants. Nothing, absolutely nothing justifies the passionate displeasure and bitter, spiteful gloom which so many have mistaken for holiness. Of what use, he asks so often, is all this self-scrutiny, this self-torture?

The man who wishes to travel the route of spiritual perfection will surely strive to acquire the virtues, but he must let God keep the score. He opposes a "too ardent interest to repress faults or acquire virtues." He who is "truly attentive to please by love the Celestial lover, has neither the inclination nor the leisure to consider himself." Not only virtues but even God's choicest supernatural graces can be loved overmuch and frequently are. One must not be too eager even to advance spiritually. How unlike Newman, who somewhere wrote, "To be at ease is to be unsafe." Avoid disquiet, perform all duties suavely, calmly; trust in the *debonnairité* of God—St. Francis de Sales never tires of repeating this message.

Like Ignatius, de Sales is convinced that the surest way to perfection is to annihilate self-love, but the Salesian way does not declare open war upon the enemies of the soul; rather, it despises their attacks. The Salesian method seeks not to vanquish the foe in pitched battle but to penetrate his lines; not to overthrow obstacles directly but to turn humbly and simply from them. Nor should it be thought that St. Francis ignores the dualistic nature of man. He recognizes it, but triumphs over it in a new way. The inferior parts of man are treated as tiresome, somewhat absurd inmates who are rendered harmless most quickly by being ignored, like exterior temptations. What we say to the "carnal man" is simply this: why, this is not even ourselves, let us forget him, let us contemptuously ignore whatever he suggests.

Implicit in the Salesian program is an unashamed optimism —but not a naive one. It is much the same optimism which many critics have noticed (and complained of) in the lyrics of Crashaw. St. Francis is convinced that there is a secret but absolute correspondence between Divine Goodness and human souls. Why else does man feel that certain, sweet, inward emotion testifying that God is God of the human heart? The state of human nature may not be endowed with its original health and rectitude, but the natural inclination to love God remains as well as the natural light by which we recognize his sovereign Goodness and overwhelming love for mankind. This natural impulse God implanted in all hearts, for He wants all men to be united to Him forever.

And if St. Francis has so little to say about sin, it is because sin is so easy to get rid of. A remedy is always at hand. Like the lioness who, after copulating with a leopard, washes herself fast to get rid of the stench, we should cleanse ourselves of sin out of love for God. The process is so easy; there is no excuse for staying long in that bottomless pit.

That great historian of religious sensibility, the Abbé Brémond, considers the Salesian devotional approach to be not only a departure from the dominant trend of the day, one which both Ignatius de Loyola and John Calvin had done much to foster, but also a completely original attitude. The voice of St. Francis de Sales is a distinctly new one.[24] The same serene detachment typifies Crashaw. Hardly a book or article treating Crashaw fails to remark how startling it is to find a seventeenth-century religious poet unconcerned with assessing his spiritual progress, taking little interest in sin, and not even interested in describing his own relationship to God.

And death, that favorite topic of seventeenth-century devotional literature, is almost absent from Crashaw's poems, as is preoccupation with sin and damnation. That "metaphysical shudder," which seems such an integral part of the flavor of seventeenth-century religious literature, is rare in Crashaw. For Crashaw, as for St. Francis, the death of the body is not very significant, being merely the passage from an imperfect union to a perfect one. Ordinarily, Crashaw, like St. Francis, uses "death" to refer to the annihilation of self-love. Only five times does the "metaphysical shudder" occur. There is a hint of it in stanza XX of "The Weeper" (1652 ed.); in "Upon Lazarus His Teares," in "The World loved darknesse more than Light," and in "Ad Judaeos mactatores S. Stephani;" there is one full-blown example, worth quoting as perhaps the most atypical (in temper) of Crashaw's religious poems:

Divine Epigram VI

> Euge, Deus—pleno populus fremit unique plausu—
> Certe non hominem vox sonat, euge, Deus!
> Sed tamen iste Deus qui sit, vos dicite, vermes,
> Intima turba illi; vos fovet ille sinu.[25]

Realizing that it is inaccurate to describe Crashaw's religious attitude as typically Spanish, French, or Italian (as opposed to English), recent critics have tended to attribute this special quality of Crashaw's religious lyrics to ritualistic or liturgical influences. D. J. Enright's article "George Herbert and the Devotional Poets" represents what has become the common view. Mr. Enright remarks that the modern reader of Crashaw does not complain, finally, of over-excitedness, but of the opposite. The individual beads are highly colored, but the hands that move them are cold and mechanical. The typical Crashaw poem is a "formal, public act of worship." [26]

I shall have occasion, as this chapter proceeds, to challenge many of these assertions, which, taken together, represent contemporary opinion quite ably. And yet Mr. Enright, together with many recent critics, shows a perceptiveness far superior to that of most critics of the recent past in realizing that Crashaw, in the final analysis, is typically relaxed, and paradoxically aloof and controlled even at his most rhapsodical. Crashaw does indeed sound notes quite distinct from those of his compatriots (and for those more than superficially acquainted with the European Baroque, quite distinct from those of poets such as Marino), but it is not the passionate, fiery, much less the mystical elements which separate him from the mainstream of English devotional writing of the period. All these elements can be found, and in an even more intense form, in some of his Puritan contemporaries. No, what marks him off is this particular *combination* of qualities: lack of preoccupation with self, sin, and death; mystical fervor tempered by a strange, almost cool aloofness; and considerable intellectual control even in the midst of the most buoyant, rhapsodical passages.

But to ascribe the final product emerging from this combination of qualities *in toto* to the ritualistic and liturgical influences is to mistake a secondary influence for the major one. There is no attempt here to gainsay the significance of the liturgical element in Crashaw, an aspect of his work which deserves serious consideration, although the scope of this study excludes it. But a far greater influence on Crashaw (and on some of his European contemporaries) was the Salesian spirituality and the Salesian method of meditation. How discouraging these were to the seventeenth-century preoccupations with self-scrutiny, death, and sin has been amply demonstrated. Salesian optimism, based on God's overwhelming love for man, turned the mind upward to contemplate God and His heaven, not inward to scrutinize self, much less downward to contemplate the worms.

From this Salesian stress on the overwhelming love of God for man, certain other doctrines flow almost as corollaries, one of which seems to have influenced Crashaw. On the controversy between free will and God's knowledge and grace, St. Francis embraced the position which moved as far away from St. Augustine as an orthodox Catholic one could without falling into Pelagianism—the doctrine of Molina. The event that led to this sudden conviction is worth noting, for it seems to have equipped him in a special way to deal with the most central problems in the devotional life of his times. As a student in Paris, Francis, an anxious, intense adolescent given to morbid introspection and scrupulosity, grew convinced that he was doomed to everlasting damnation. But once as he knelt despairing in the Church of St. Etienne des Gres, praying the Memorare before the "Black Virgin," a celebrated statue of Mary, a sudden conviction of election, or more specifically, a sudden assurance of God's love for him, put an end to these torments. The young theological student seems to have experienced something akin to the "religious conversion" in the fundamental Protestant sense. In a sense, St. Francis de Sales became convinced that he was "saved." So it is no accident that his advice seems so perfectly calculated to calm the tortured consciences of his time, and no accident that he knew so well how to reach the minds and hearts of the Calvinists of Chablais.

It costs him much to separate himself from the Thomistic-Augustinian position on Predestination, but he did so unhesitatingly. To the Jesuit theologian, Père Lessius, he wrote a friendly letter, assuring him that he has always regarded the Molinistic doctrine on Predestination as the one most in accord with God's love and mercy.[27] This Molinistic doctrine is amplified in the *Traité* with superb clarity. While it is true that heavenly grace is needed before man can take even one step in God's direction, and although this grace, because of the principle of plenitude, is granted to men in widely varying degrees, it is nonetheless lavished superabundantly even on the least fortunate of God's children. But the grace of God is never irresistible. Respecting the essential nature of his creature, God leaves a man free to reject even His most priceless graces. In no way, Francis insists again and again, can it be said that God's grace compels. But, alas, man, through his perversity, can and so often does reject divine graces, or at least fails to use them wisely. Thus the blame for sin is man's entirely, for failing to use wisely God's superabundant graces. And while it is true that dying in the state of grace is a gift (final perseverance) it is granted as a reward for having made at least reasonably good use of heavenly graces; it is denied as a punishment for having too often spurned God's choicest graces. God foresees who will cooperate with Him and who will spurn Him, and distributes heavenly gifts accordingly.

In this view God emerges as neither a tyrant nor an arbitrary Power whose ways are, above all, *completely* inscrutable. Somewhat mysterious He remains, but His role is not unsimilar to that of a benign, gracious schoolmaster who wishes all of his students to pass the course. He makes of them only a few sane, moderate requirements, lavishes aids and exhortations, and assures them that, if they put forth a reasonable effort, he will do the rest. But through sheer recalcitrance some students simply *will not* do their homework, even after many warnings. Alas, what remains for the schoolmaster at the end of the term but tearfully to write "Fail" on the report cards? This Molinistic point of view, obviously, sets a high premium on the freedom of man's will. To God is given the greater glory, for His grace is necessary from the start; but to man, too, whose free, generous cooperation plays such a significant role, one can at least say, "Well done, good and faithful servant." His master has given him the necessary tools, but he has made splendid use of them. It should be immediately apparent how appealing such a view must have been to Renaissance humanists. One has nothing to fear from God, then; one need fear only his own perverse refusal to cooperate with superabundant graces. St. Francis de Sales, we recall, terms this view the most "comforting" doctrine, a statement based upon his faith not only in the ineffable goodness of God but also in the essential goodness of His fallen creatures.

Crashaw, too, seems to have embraced the Bishop's theology, the Molinistic view on Predestination. Some might point to Crashaw's obvious celebration of the human element in the spiritual triumphs of the Magdalen and St. Teresa of Avila, but a more striking example of what appears to be an overt rejection of Augustinian Predestination (to which the Anglican Church was officially committed) occurs in his translation of the medieval Latin hymn "Dies Irae." Crashaw's translation of this hymn follows the original Latin more closely than most of his translations do, and his changes are usually by way of expansion or embellishment. But in one stanza, and only in one stanza, he departs radically from the *meaning* of the original. Stanza XVII of the Latin Hymn reads as follows:

> Rex tremendae majestatis,
> Qui salvandos salvas gratis
> Salva me, fons pietatis.[28]

The Augustinian overtones of the stanza did not ring pleasantly in Crashaw's ears, for he translates:

> But Thou giv'st leave (dread Lord!) that we
> Take shelter from Thyself, in Thee;
> And with the wings of Thine Own dove
> Fly to Thy scepter of soft Love.

It is the implications of the Latin gerundive *salvandos* which apparently made our poet somewhat uneasy. He utterly avoids this turn of thought, and not for any obvious technical exigencies. Instead he chooses to elaborate the *fons pietatis*, strengthening the comfort this phrase affords by expanding it or, rather, by converting it to "Fly to Thy scepter of soft love," although he is cautious enough to underline the role which grace plays even in the first step of turning to God for assistance, with the phrase "And with the wings of thine Own dove." If one were not aware of the theological issues involved, how easy it would be to say that Crashaw has diluted the stark masculinity of the medieval hymn with Baroque preciosity and embellishment.

Crashaw's God is the God of ineffable love, first and foremost, and the reader is never permitted to forget that. Thus between stanzas XI and XII of the original Crashaw inserts a stanza of his own, not to bridge the thought between the Latin stanzas XI and XII, in which case his addition would

be an improvement, but perhaps because he felt ill at ease
with such lines as these:

> Mercy (my Judge) mercy I cry
> With blushing cheek and bleeding ey:
> The conscious colors of my sin
> Are red without and pale within.

The Latin version goes on in the next stanza to remind Christ
that by having absolved Mary Magdalen and the Penitent
Thief on the Cross He has given hope to the suppliant faithful. And Crashaw will follow this Latin text almost literally,
but not yet. First he must greatly expand the role of God as
lover of mankind, even though to do so he must alter the
structure of the original by interposing a stanza of his own
(stanza XII in Crashaw's version):

> O let Thine Own soft bowells pay
> Thyself; and so discharge that day.
> If Sin can sigh, Love can forgive:
> O say the word, my soul shall live.

The original poet, it seems, did not sufficiently stress God's
love for his fallen creatures. Nor, St. Francis de Sales would
have maintained, have most devotional writers and spiritual
counsellors.

But to regard the Salesian way as thorn-free and smooth is
to misunderstand it utterly—and with it Crashaw. St. Francis
de Sales does not ask his spiritual charges to apply a scalpel
to their psyches, to engage in agonizing self-scrutiny. Nor
does he ask them to smell the brimstone of Hell or to imagine
the slimy touch of the coffin worm. No, he spares them all this
—but only to make a far more brutal demand of them. What
he requires is a frightening mortification of the will, an

unequivocal surrender of self. Upon this strict conformity
of man's will to God's no one has insisted more persistently,
more ruthlessly than he. It is just as much a part of the Salesian way as are the refreshing optimism and what Butler calls
his "sweet reasonableness." [29]

To maintain the serenity which St. Francis demands often
involves the harshest self-discipline, as does his request that
his spiritual charges live in such a manner as to be a source of
annoyance to no one. It is amazing how closely related the
virtues of charity and affability often are to fortitude! But
especially difficult is the dying unto oneself. One must accept
gladly, calmly, whatever God sends. However, God's will
need not always be opposed to man's; and it is imprudent
to volunteer for tribulations. To desire for yourself nothing
except what God desires—this is spiritual perfection.

It is precisely this self-surrender to God, with the excruciating mortification of the individual will which it involves,
that Crashaw celebrates in "The Weeper" and in the St.
Teresa poems. The poet understands well what the Heavenly
Spouse demands of His bride, for the spiritual life of the
Spanish mystic is referred to as "milder martyrdom" (Line
68 in "A Hymn to the Admirable Sainte Teresa"), and the
basic meaning of the elaborate passage beginning with "O
how oft shalt thou complain/ Of a sweet and subtle pain,"
followed by the celebrated life-death paradoxes (96–106), is
that the human partner in the divine romance must surrender his individual will to God, dying unto himself the most
painful of all deaths. This he does joyfully, for it is in this
way that he achieves the closest possible union with the
Heavenly Lover; and, paradoxically, one's individuality,
after the union, is not lost, but returned—enhanced. Crashaw
is at his very best when he celebrates the painful annihilation
of self-love and the ineffable reward which results.

It is a mistake to regard Crashaw as a naive, easy-going optimist who celebrates an undemanding, sentimental, buoyant spirituality. No seventeenth-century poet is more aware than he that sweat and tears are an integral part of the mystical experience. It is not for nothing that we read so often about "darts," "wounds," "blood," "deaths." These are meant to remind us that self-love dies a death both slow and hard. To surrender the will completely is to endure excruciating pains; it is no easy task to discipline oneself to desire nothing but what God desires. It is a process frightening to contemplate, this self-surrender. What a sad mistake it is to look upon the dart and wound imagery which honeycombs Crashaws devotional works as exercises in preciosity at best, masochism at worst. It serves to remind us, rather, of the harshest realities of the Christian life. But Crashaw sees beyond the painful annihilation of self-love to the ineffable reward which results, his celebration of which has no equal in English poetry.

Not only theme and attitude but Crashaw's imagery, as well, were influenced by Salesian writings, especially by the richly imagistic *Introduction to a Devout Life*. To try to trace Crashaw's imagery to any one source is usually a futile attempt. The Bible, the Spanish mystics (St. Teresa much more than St. John of the Cross), Dionysius the Areopagite, Chapman and Herbert—all these merge, reinforcing and modifying each other, and become, finally, largely inextricable. Nor should it be too easily assumed, as it often is, that a writer is conscious of the source of his imagery. This study claims only that the prose of St. Francis de Sales is one of several significant influences that helped shape Crashaw's imagery. Only rarely is it possible to ascertain, even with a moderate degree of probability, whether a given passage in St. Francis is the prime source of a group of images in a

Crashaw poem, or whether that Salesian passage acted merely as a minor, reinforcing agent.

Several qualities of Crashaw's imagery set him apart from other major seventeenth-century English devotional poets; one of these is his lavish use of images appealing to the senses of smell and taste. In fact, the delights of the palate and nostril are Crashaw's favorite way of symbolizing spiritual satisfactions, heavenly rejoicings, and acceptability to God. In spite of Biblical precedent for the use of such imagery, the occidental world has rarely been much inclined to use it extensively. There is, as Mary Ewer tells us, an insidious conviction that physical delights of palate and nostril are unworthy of mankind, that they belong to a subhuman order, and thus are not worthy to symbolize spiritual things. The Orientals alone seem really at home with this type of imagery.[30]

St. Francis, too, has an un-occidental penchant for such imagery. Much of the *Devout Life* is drenched in honey and saturated with exotic perfumes. Only one characteristic passage will be quoted here, for the reader can turn at random to almost any page to find many more. This one reads like prose renditions of a poem Crashaw might easily have written:

> The skies, sings the Church, from all sides pour down honey, and to my fancy those Angels whose marvelous songs are still resounding through the air, may descend to gather that heavenly honey from the Lily where it lies, on the bosom of the Sweetest Virgin, with St. Joseph. I fear, my dear daughter, that these divine spirits might mistake the milk flowing from the virginal breast for the heavenly honey with which that breast has been anointed.[31]

Honey and bees are St. Francis' favorite images. On numerous occasions he turns to them to construct little emblem-

atic devices to convey spiritual truth; from these a basic
pattern emerges. The bees, invariably, represent those devout
souls earnestly engaged in leading the Christ-life; the flowers
symbolize something numinous—prayer, dogma, spiritual
books, heavenly inspirations; the honey is an analogue for
whatever results from the contact between the devout soul
and the numinous object. Thus, St. Francis tells Philothea
that neophytes in the art of mental prayer should depend
upon spiritual books to suggest the most fruitful points of
meditation, just as nymphs (immature bees), unable to make
their own food, must feed upon the honey provided by mature bees. Crashaw creates a variation of his own in this general emblematic pattern:

> "To the Name Above Every Name" (151–158)
>
> Lo, where A loft it comes! it comes, Among
> The conduct of adoring Spirits, that throng
> Like diligent Bees, and swarm about it.
>   O they are wise;
> And know what SWEETS are suck't from out it.
>   It is the Hive,
>   By which they thrive,
> Where all their Hoard of Hony lyes.

Like Crashaw, St. Francis is fond of using gems to symbolize preciousness, and the Bishop of Geneva is a possible
source for Crashaw's breast and nest imagery. St. Francis
alludes rather freely, even for his age, to breasts—of mothers
and of the Virgin Mary. For instance, God, in one passage, is
compared to a mother who smears honey on her breasts to
lure her infants. In another passage *nest* and *breast* are com-
bined in a manner highly reminiscent of Crashaw:

Now it is true, dear sister and daughter, that my body was somewhat tired after the procession, but how could my mind and heart have been so, after I carried on my breast and united my heart with so divine an anthem, as I have done this morning throughout the procession! "The sparrow has found herself a house and the swallow a nest where she may lay her young," says David. My God, how I was touched when they chanted that psalm! For I meditated, "Oh dear Queen of Heaven, *is it possible that your Nestling has now my breast for its nest*. This word of the Spouse has moved me: "My beloved is mine; he dwells between my breasts; for I bore Him there." [32] (italics mine)

It is quite probable, incidentally, that Crashaw had an opportunity to read the letters of St. Francis. In 1626, four years after the death of St. Francis, his nephew Louis de Sales published an edition of the letters at Lyons. So popular did this edition prove that a second revised version followed two years later. Now this edition, in turn, was reprinted more than forty times in the course of the seventeenth century and circulated widely throughout Europe. It seems reasonable to assume that Crashaw, upon whom Salesian doctrine made such a profound impression, would have made at least an ordinary effort to secure a copy of these highly popular letters.

The imagery of the Song of Songs appears often in both the *Introduction to a Devout Life* and the *Traité*, but St. Francis' use was most likely merely a reinforcing agent, except for the development of the wound of love imagery, already discussed in this chapter.

Much more than a reinforcing agent, though, was the Salesian method of meditation, which differs in some significant ways from the Ignatian. Now, it was the Ignatian method in its many modified forms that had by far the greater influence evident not only in Bishop Hall's *Arte of Divine Meditation* but even in Baxter's discussions of meditation. Louis Martz is quite right in stressing the influence of the Ignation "composition of place" on English devotional poetry. But it was Julius Locke who first pointed out that the lyrics of Crashaw, unlike devotional works such as "The Burning Babe" (wherein Ignatian particularity is so evident), do not seem to have been much influenced by this dominant devotional trend.[33] A meditative tradition quite different from the one which influenced most of his compatriots lies behind much of Crashaw's work and is far more responsible than has been realized for some of those elements which we regard as typically Crashaw.

It seems necessary, then, to describe the Salesian method of meditation, demonstrating its departures from the Ignatian. Conventionally enough, St. Francis recommends as a first step that the meditator place himself in the presence of God, but he puts unusual stress on this point. Placing oneself in the presence of God involves more than ridding oneself of worldly distractions: it requires a lively, attentive apprehension of the divine presence in every object in the visible environment.[34] A magic wand, so to speak, must strike every object near the meditator, charging it with spiritual significance, transforming it into an icon. The second step requires the meditator to invoke God's assistance.

It is the third step which differs most substantially from the Ignatian method. In the Salesian method, one proposes, formally, the subject of the mystery he intends to meditate on, but the "composition of place" is arbitrary. We look in vain for that extensive application of the senses and for the encouragement of strong, even violent emotions that typify the Ignatian method. Instead, St. Francis warns the meditator that even if he does find it useful to picture mentally a given scene, he should not spend much time visualizing elaborate, exact detail. He fears that the meditator may pervert the devotional exercise by "searching out curious inventions," and thus disturb the "tranquillity" of his mind. In any case, the Salesian composition of place pales almost into insignificance when contrasted with the Ignatian.

This is not to say that the Salesian method frowns on mental icons. St. Francis would hardly have disagreed with St. Thomas Aquinas, who in the *Summa Theologica* (I. lxxxxxiv.7) tells us that intellectual ideas formed in the mind (about God) are not really understood by the intellect unless they are turned to images (*ad phantasmata*) so that the mind may behold the universal in the particular, wherein alone it has real existence. Nevertheless, St. Francis insists that it is better to conceive of heavenly things in as spiritual a manner as possible, although many concessions must be made to beginners. He would not have agreed, surely, with the Jesuit Gibbons, who tells us that we must use the image-forming faculty to provide for as concrete and vivid a setting as possible for the meditation on invisible things.[35] This is not the Salesian way.

After the (optional) act of imagination, there follows the act of the understanding or the meditation proper, which "consists in making reflections and considerations in order to raise up our affections to God and heavenly things." Now this fourth step is not to be confused with study or hard intellectual exercise. Intellectual operations play a much less significant role than in the Ignatian method. The purpose of the Salesian meditation is to produce pious motions in the will or "affective part of our soul, such as the love of God and neighbor, desire of heaven and eternal glory, zeal for salvation of souls, imitation of the life of our Lord, compassion, admiration, joy. . . ." The role of the intellect, then, is to propose points and to analyze them, but unless there is a spillover to the volitional and affective "parts of the soul," the meditation has not been successful. As for dogmatic controversy, this should never be the subject of one's meditation. "By temperament" de Sales hates those theological contentions which led nowhere except to slander and destruction of charity.

During the course of the meditation, "OUR HEARTS SHOULD EXPAND AS MUCH AS POSSIBLE" (capitals mine). To meditate is not to prepare mentally an organized lecture on a spiritual topic. The purpose is to propose points that will move the will and emotions in the direction of God. Thus, there need be no particular plan. One should move at random like a bee; if a particular flower (point of meditation) does not please, one should move on calmly to another point. But should some particular blossom be especially delightful, then let the meditator remain there to suck nectar as long as he wishes. What counts is that there be honey produced (spiritual profit), not that some organizational scheme be faithfully followed. Thus, "IT IS A GENERAL RULE NEVER TO RESTRAIN THE AFFECTIONS BUT TO LET THEM HAVE THEIR FREE COURSE WHENEVER THEY PRESENT THEMSELVES." One should be free, during the meditation, to follow the inner promptings of the heart, wherever these may lead. Should yearnings to offer prayers of thanksgiving or to offer oneself to God arise, these should be satisfied. But one impulse, and only this one, is to be restrained. The meditator must never make particular resolutions or engage in self-scrutiny during the meditation proper, for such "particularity" is bound to distract him and rivet his attention not on God but on himself.

The Salesian method of meditation, then, encourages an unusual degree of freedom, and does not insist upon strict logical development. One need not move quickly from point B to point C if point B is particularly fruitful and suggestive; on the other hand, one is free to omit point B and proceed from A directly to C should B seem profitless. And nothing prevents one from returning to A after contemplating C, should one feel an impulse to do so. In fact, the only impulse one need restrain is one which would militate against the theocentric nature of the Salesian meditation, that is, of the meditation proper (as distinct from the conclusion).

Before discussing the last steps in the Salesian meditation, we should qualify this emphasis on the "expansion of the heart." St. Francis de Sales does not encourage the stimulating of passionate, much less wildly ecstatic, emotions. A "too great tenderness," he warns, disquiets and distracts the heart from prayerful adoration of God. Step five in the Salesian method is the making of a highly particular resolution, this being part of the conclusion (as distinct from the meditation proper). The meditator should make arrangements to put into practice the virtue he has contemplated. After the resolution he should thank God for His inspirations, offer the resolutions up to Him, begging for help in carrying them out. Finally, and this last point is original with St. Francis, the meditator should fashion for himself a spiritual nosegay. Just as one who walks in a beautiful garden does not depart willingly without gathering a few flowers to smell during the remainder of the day, so the devout meditator ought to select a point or two which he has most relished for reminiscence later in the day. He ought frequently to "smell" of it "spiritually."

Both the organization of Crashaw's lyrics and the nature of their imagery were substantially influenced by this method of meditation. Most of his longer poems commence with a direct announcement of the subject matter proposed for meditation. "Hail, sister springs!" exclaims the poet-meditator, proposing the supernatural repentance of Mary Magdalen as his theme. "O these wakefull wounds of thine!" ("On the Wounds of Our Crucified Lord") and "Rise, Heir of fresh Eternity" ("Easter Day"), "Love, thou are absolute sole Lord of life and death" ("In Memory of the Vertuous and Learned Lady Madre de Teresa") are more than introductory phrases. They announce the general theme for meditation and implicit in them are most of the subsequent developments of the lyric. In the same category are:

> "Thus have I back again to thy bright name
> (Fair floud of holy fires!) transfus'd the flame
> I took from reading thee" ("An Apologie")
> and "I sing the name which none can say
> But touch't with an interior Ray"
> ("To the Name above Every Name").

The fourth step had a much greater influence, with its encouragement of the leisurely musing on a point, moving on to another when that is exhausted, returning to an earlier point if one feels so inclined. The purpose is to excite pious sentiments and firm movements of the will toward God. Thus, like a bee, the meditator sucks as much nectar as possible from each blossom. The meditative thought is to proceed slowly, calmly, seizing upon those points which seem most "to expand the heart." The line of development is basically firm, in fact, usually logical, for the relationship between the points proposed for meditation is rational. It is never difficult to see *why* a given thought occurs, if the reader is aware that he is reading a poetic meditation. Obviously, the line of development is never inevitable, for no two meditations on the same subject are, or should be, identical.

Chapter III will demonstrate how in "The Weeper" the poet-meditator muses on point after point concerning the Magdalen's repentance, now returning to an earlier point, now suddenly perceiving new implications, new relationships between the points, now merging several points into one—"It is a general rule never to restrain the affections but to let them have their free course whenever they present themselves." Crashaw heeded this warning well, as he did the admonition to admit no self-scrutiny, no particularity into the body of the meditation. And passionate excitement is not typical of Crashaw. There is firm control, even in those highly rhapsodic moments, as Willey noticed when he characterized Crashaw's prevailing mood as "at once inflamed and relaxed." [36]

The divine epigrams, too, are basically meditative in nature, although each proposes only one point. To impress that one point firmly on the mind of the reader, to prevent its evoking a stock response (to be avoided even more in meditative poetry than in secular), all the ingenuity of the poet is pressed into service. Such is the purpose of the piling up of startling paradoxes in the epigram "Verily I say unto you, yee shall weep and lament":

> . . . Welcome my Griefe, my Joy; how deare's
> To me my legacy of Teares!
> I'le weepe, and weepe, and will therefore
> Weepe, 'cause I can weepe no more:
> Thou, thou (deare Lord) even thou alone
> Giv'st joy, even when thou givest none.

Startling antitheses, bizarre images, preciosity, keep epigrammatic point—with what new and fresh light we flood this rhetorical ingenuity by considering it as a means to "expand the heart" and "raise the affections up to God." The technical requirements of this genre harmonize beautifully with the ends of a verse meditation; there is mutual enhancement.

Mary Ewer reminds us that "Human language has been formed in the stress of sense experience." [37] Thus, if spiritual experiences are to be communicated poetically, the poet has little choice but to express himself through some sort of analogy, through images. But there are at least two ways in which these verbal icons could conceivably be used. The poet may use sensuous particulars like so many points comprising an emotional and imagistic route to a basically cognitive goal. In other words, he may expect the reader to respond emotionally to the image and then rise above it to grasp a concept. Crashaw uses imagery in this manner rarely. The Ignatian method of meditation lends itself to such a use of imagery.

Typically, however, Crashaw uses images in a different manner, the emotional response being elicited not by the icon, however sensuous, but directly by the idea embodied therein. And if the sensuousness of many of the symbols distracts the reader, this is simply because for him the spiritual experience seems vaguer than its imagistic representation. To the poet-meditator, however, it is the mystical experience that is clear and vigorous, while its sensuous analogue is merely a weak, woefully inadequate attempt to portray the spiritual experience. Especially is this true of erotic imagery.

Thus it is (as Crashaw's most perceptive critics have noted) that the imagery of a typical Crashaw poem strikes the reader as sensuous perhaps but also curiously unreal. Locke overstates his case badly in asserting that the Crashaw image is *never* material, but ordinarily Crashaw's imagery does indeed lack "the immediacy of an empirical organization of sense imagery." [38] Precisely; Crashaw's imagery does indeed lack this sensuous immediacy, but it has *spiritual* immediacy. However, I disagree with Locke's suggestion that a *contemptus mundi* is the reason for the otherworldly nature of the imagery. Crashaw's images are symbols aimed at a direct presentation of spiritual experience. The Salesian method of meditation is surely one that would encourage just this use of imagery. The composition of place (as has been shown) is optional with St. Francis and, even when introduced, is used sparingly. In Crashaw's lyrics there is little trace of this meditative technique. His meditations have no particular setting. St. Francis, one recalls, encouraged the conceiving of heavenly topics in as spiritual a manner as possible. And Crashaw, the poet-meditator, is concerned, typically, with spiritual concepts; he focuses his attention directly on these. The images appear disembodied, impossible to visualize, because their purpose is purely ideational.

Wylie Sypher is surely wrong in complaining that Crashaw first exalts and then naively adores his images.[39] Had Crashaw done so, he might have been a better poet; for when he goes astray, he does so precisely because he is so absorbed in a spiritual concept that he *ignores* the icon, which, it must never be forgotten, is the only means he has to lift most of us up to this rarefied atmosphere.

One must be cautious also in speaking of Crashaw's successful striving to transcend the material realm. Crashaw does not *strive*. The transcendence is a *fait accompli* even as the poem begins. We are already in a spiritual realm where no image has its face value. The typical Crashaw lyric does not so much propel us into heavenly realms as assume we are already there. There is perhaps some connection between this characteristic and St. Francis' urgings to "practice frequently the presence of God," before meditating and even at other times as an exercise in its own right. St. Francis suggests that

Philothea look at every object around her, empty it of all
but its spiritual significance, as did St. Francisca, who, while
contemplating a brook, remarked, "The grace of God flows
thus gently and sweetly like this little stream." This is precisely what has happened to the *typical* Crashaw image; it
has been emptied of all but its spiritual significance, not
gradually during the course of the poem, but even before
being pressed into service.

The emblem, which, long before Crashaw's use of it, was
already associated in the popular mind with meditation and
devotional exercises, served the needs of the meditative lyric
particularly well. Our poet could use it in many ways: to
pack away a wealth of doctrine into one image; to expand a
thought or arouse the mind to a richer appreciation of it by
imagistic embellishment; even to repeat a thought for emphasis by embodying it in a novel, lush image to entice the
reader to dwell on the concept therein embodied. Mary Ellen
Rickey suggests that Crashaw's repetitive devices can be attributed to the influence of the long, topical lyric; a more
significant influence is the meditative nature of the religious
lyric.[40] Thus we find Crashaw usually busy at one of two
tasks, the first analytic, the second synthetic. Typically, he
either introduces an emblematic picture ready made for pious, meditative analysis; or, at his most skillful, slowly, ingeniously arranges his own symbols into an emblematic device, whose meaning emerges gradually as its parts are
assembled.

The religious sensibility, favorite images, and meditative
method of St. Francis de Sales, the emblematic tradition of
the earlier seventeenth century, the Elizabethan and Jacobean
poetic heritage—if these streams were suddenly to converge,
the result would be poetry much like Crashaw's.

NOTES

[1] Helen C. White, *English Devotional Literature: Prose, 1600–1640,* in *University of Wisconsin Studies in Language and Literature,* No. 19 (Madison, Wisconsin; 1931), p. 49.

[2] White, p. 89.

[3] Quoted in E. I. Watkin, *Poets and Mystics* (London, 1954), pp. 55–56.

[4] *Ibid.*

[5] William Crashaw, "A Sermon preached in London before the Right Honourable the Lord Lavvarre, Lord Governour and Captaine Generall of Virginea, and others of His Majesties Counsell for that Kingdome, and the rest of the adventurers in that plantation" (London, printed for W. Welby, 1610). Running title on mircofilm is "A New Yeeres Gift to Virginea."

[6] Richard Baxter, *A Christian Directory, or a Sum of Practical Theology and Cases of Conscience in Four Parts,* Vol. III, *Christian Ecclesiastics,* ed. Orme (London, 1830), p. 266.

[7] *Christian Ecclesiastics,* p. 593.

[8] Louis Martz, *The Poetry of Meditation* (Yale, 1956), p. 114.

[9] Richard Baxter, *The Saints Everlasting Rest,* ed. Eddowes (London, 1768), p. 286.

[10] Francis Rous, "The Mysticall Marriage. Experimentall discoveries of the heavenly marriage betweene a soule and her Saviour" (London, printed by Jones, 1631).

[11] Quoted by Watkin, p. 142.

[12] *Devotional Prose,* pp. 111–113.

[13] Anthony F. Allison, "Crashaw and St. François de Sales," *RES,* XIV (Oct. 1948), pp. 295–302.

[14] See *Traité de l'Amour de Dieu* (Paris, 1925), pp. 238–244 for the specific source of Crashaw's lines. (All translations mine)

[15] *Traité,* p. 96.

[16] St. Francis de Sales, *Introduction to the Devout Life,* trans. and ed. John K. Ryan (New York, 1956), p. 21. The best way to get at the Salesian spirit quickly is to read pages 56–58 of the *Traité.* On page 57 he discusses the proposition "Que la Providence céleste a pourvu aux hommes une rédemption tres abontante." God

loved the world so ardently that he was not content to grant man merely *sufficient* means for salvation; instead, he has lavished upon him such superabundant means that one marvels that anyone could miss salvation.

[17] *Selected Letters of St. Francis de Sales,* ed. and trans. Elisabeth Stopp (New York, 1960), p. 67.

[18] The explication of Salesian theology which follows draws from all of de Sales' extant writings, especially *The Introduction, The Traité,* and the *Letters.* All works have been assembled in one collection: *Oeuvres Completes de St. François de Sales,* ed. Dom Mackey (Lyon, 1923), XII, an edition begun in 1892.

[19] Arno Esch, *Englische Religiöse Lyrik des 17 Jahrhundert* (Tübingen, 1955), p. 97.

[20] Once again His love will glow with yours,

once again His tears will flow with yours;

you will be present at His cradle, at His burial,

and be witness to burning loves, including mine.

(All translations of Crashaw's Latin and Greek poems are mine.)

[21] The leprosy which was once in the body now spreads over (literally, *sits in*) the soul. A change has occurred and *justly* so; they are now as distant from God as they once were from men.

[22] *Oeuvres,* XII, p. 333. (All translations mine)

[23] *Oeuvres,* VI, p. 419.

[24] Henri Brémond, *Histoire Littéraire du Sentiment Réligieux en France* (Paris, 1923), Vol. I, p. 113.

[25] Behold a god! so the people cry out with full applause, Surely, he's no man but a God rather, so their voices proclaim him. But tell us, oh ye worms, what kind of God is he? Tell us, oh crowd (of worms) now so intimate with him, you whom he nourishes with his breast.

[26] D. J. Enright, "George Herbert and the Devotional Poets," in *From Donne to Marvell,* ed. Boris Ford (Baltimore, 1962), pp. 158–159.

[27] See *Brémond,* p. 91.

[28] O King of tremendous majesty,/ Oh you who save *freely* those *who are* (destined) *to be saved* (italics mine)/Save me, oh fountain of pity. *The St. Andrew Daily Missal,* ed. Lefebvre (St. Paul, Minnesota; 1945), pp. 1798–1800.

[29] Cuthbert Butler, *Ways of the Christian Life* (New York, 1932), p. 166.

[30] Mary Ewer, *A Survey of Mystical Symbolism* (London, 1933), p. 52.

[31] *Oeuvres*, XIV, p. 392.

[32] *Oeuvres*, XIV, p. 169. (This letter—to St. Jane de Chantal—is not included in *Selected Letters*.)

[33] Julius Locke, *Images and Image Symbolized in Metaphysical Poetry with Special Reference to Otherworldliness*, unpublished dissertation (University of Florida, Gainesville; 1958); see esp. pp. 95–96.

[34] de Sales discusses meditation in the *Introduction to the Devout Life* (trans. & ed. John Ryan, New York, 1956), pp. 67–74.

[35] Quoted and discussed by Martz, p. 26.

[36] Quoted by Enright, pp. 158–159.

[37] Ewer, p. 27.

[38] Locke, p. 79.

[39] Wylie Sypher, *Four Stages of Renaissance Style* (New York, 1956), p. 238.

[40] Mary Ellen Rickey, *Rhyme and Meaning in Crashaw* (Lexington, Kentucky, 1961), p. 26.

A NEW LOOK AT
THE WEEPER

A Baroque Verse Meditation in Salesian Mode

Perhaps no English Baroque poem offends twentieth-century taste quite so much as "The Weeper." Two obstacles militate against a modern appreciation of this lyric. Critics have usually found the structure of Crashaw's lyrics puzzling, but especially that of "The Weeper" and "To the Name above Every Name." Perhaps the most thorough study of the structure of Crashaw's religious lyrics is the recent one of Arno Esch, who sees the poem as an incoherent stringing together of pious thoughts, a formless grouping of highly colored beads. In general, Crashaw's sympathetic critics, who find other reasons to admire the poem, accept that judgment. (A notable exception is Stephen Manning, although I cannot accept his reading of the poem as an exposition of the spiritual life, based on St. Teresa.) This chapter proposes that "The Weeper" has been modeled on the method of formal meditation developed and popularized by St. Francis de Sales. Read as a formal Salesian meditation, "The Weeper" takes on a firm, actually predictable structure, and even the grotesqueries of the poem, to a great degree, emerge as esthetically justifiable. This Salesian substructure is evident in many other of Crashaw's religious lyrics, especially in the "To the Name above Every Name." And it is applicable also to a fair number of devotional poems written in the Puritan camp in the mid-seventeenth century. A close look at the Puritan poetry in Perry Miller's anthology—with my thesis in mind —will reveal amazing similarities between Crashaw and the Puritans.

The other obstacle to a modern appreciation of "The Weeper," and perhaps an even more formidable one, is the near-universal view that Crashaw, in certain poems, seems merely to repeat the same concept over and over in different images, a habit usually attributed to the baroque love for dramatic emphasis and luxurious amplitude. Even generous critics generally regard these "iterative" images as essentially different from the intellectual conceits occurring in poems or in passages which develop concepts in a straightforward, logical, relatively terse manner.

Of all the critics of "The Weeper" Stephen Manning seems the most generous, but even he sees the opening stanza as merely an "accumulation of images" all expressing the same concept. The justification of this redundancy, supposedly, is the poet's attempt to illustrate his inadequacy to express these divine truths. This analysis hopes to demonstrate that almost *no* image is truly redundant, that although the poet embodies the same *basic* concept in several images, he significantly modifies the sense with each turn of the image. When Crashaw repeats, it is with a significant difference.

An analysis of "The Weeper" seems the best way to tie together the strands of this book and thus provide support compelling enough to stimulate serious reexamination of standard critical opinion. Two other explications of "The Weeper" are extant. Stephen Manning's interpretation (in "The Meaning of 'The Weeper,'" *ELH*, XXII, March 1955, 34–47) is an admirable work which recognizes emblems for what they are. For Manning "The Weeper" emerges as a study of the spiritual life, based on St. Teresa's exposition. But this conclusion is not reached without what seems to me some rather tortuous ingenuity, nor without crediting sensibility, as that is revealed by his other works. It is all very fine to insist on Crashaw's intellectuality, to offset the criticism of the past; but Crashaw is *not* Donne. In the final analysis *firm control* rather than intellectuality (much less, profundity) is the term to employ in defining the characteristic poetic method of Crashaw. The other explication is that of John Peter ("Crashaw and 'The Weeper'," *Scrutiny*, XIX, October 1958, 258–273), who seems largely unaware of the emblematic nature of the imagery, claiming instead that the *primary* purpose of Crashaw's imagery is to establish mood.[1]

This analysis of "The Weeper" is based on the 1652 version, taken from Martin's second (revised) edition, *The Poems English Latin and Greek of Richard Crashaw* (Oxford, 1957). The entire poem is reproduced here for the convenience of the reader.

THE WEEPER

I.

> Hail, sister springs!
> Parents of sylver-footed rills!
>   Ever bubbling things!
>   Thawing crystall! snowy hills,
> Still spending, never spent! I mean
> Thy fair eyes, sweet MAGDALENE!

II.

Heavens they fair eyes be;
Heavens of ever-falling starres.
'Tis seed-time still with thee
And starres thou sow'st, whose harvest dares
Promise the earth to counter shine
Whatever makes heaven's forehead fine.

III.

But we are deceived all.
Starres indeed they are too true;
For they but seem to fall,
As Heaven's other spangles doe.
It is not for our earth and us
To shine in Things so pretious.

IV.

Upwards thou dost weep.
Heaven's bosome drinks the gentle stream.
Where th'milky rivers creep,
Thine floates above; & is the cream.
Waters above th'Heavens, what they be
We' are taught best by thy TEARES & thee.

V.

Every morn from hence
A brisk Cherub somthing sippes
Whose sacred influence
Addes sweetnes to his sweetest Lippes.
Then to his musick. And his song
Tasts of this Breakfast all day long.

VI.

Not in the evening's eyes
When they Red with weeping are
For the Sun that dyes,
Sitts sorrow with a face so fair,
No where but here did ever meet
Sweetnesse so sad, sadnesse so sweet.

VII.

When sorrow would be seen
In her brightest majesty
(For she is a Queen)
Then is she drest by none but thee
Then and only then, she weares
Her proudest pearles; I mean, thy TEARES.

VIII.

The deaw no more will weep
The primrose's pale cheek to deck,
The deaw no more will sleep
Nuzzel'd in the lilly's neck;
Much reather would it be they TEAR,
And leave them Both to tremble here.

IX.

There's no need at all
That the balsom-sweating bough
So coyly should let fall
His med'cinable teares; for now
Nature hath learn't to extract a deaw
More soveraign & sweet from you.

X.

Yet let the poore drops weep
(Weeping is the ease of woe)
Softly let them creep,
Sad that they are vanquish't so.
They, though to others no releife,
Balsom maybe, for their won greife.

XI.

Such the maiden gemme
By the purpling vine put on,
Peeps from her parent stemme
And blushes at the bridegroome sun.
This watry Blossom of thy eyn,
Ripe, will make the richer wine.

XII.

When some new bright Guest
Takes up among the starres a room,
And Heavn will make a feast,
Angels with crystall violls come
And draw from these full eyes of thine
Their Masters' Water: their own Wine.

XIII.

Golden though he be,
Golden Tagus murmures tho:
Were his way by thee,
Content & Quiet he would goe.
So much more rich would he esteem
Thy sylver, then his golden stream.

XIV.

Well does the May that lyes
  Smiling in thy cheeks, confesse
The April in thine eyes.
  Mutuall sweetnesse they expresse.
No April ere lent kinder showres,
Nor May return'd more faithful flowers.

XV.

O cheeks! Bedds of chast loves
  By your own showres seasonably dash't
Eyes! nests of milky doves
  In your own wells decently washt,
O wit of love! that thus could place
Fountain & Garden in one face.

XVI.

O sweet Contest; of woes
  With loves, of teares with smiles disputing!
O fair, & freindly Foes,
  Each other kissing & confuting!
While rain & sunshine Cheekes & Eyes
Close in kind contrarietyes.

XVII.

But can these fair Flouds be
  Freinds with the bosom fires that fill thee
Can so great flames agree
  Aeternall Teares should thus distill thee!
O flouds, o fires! o suns! o showres!
Mixt & make freinds by love's sweet powres.

XVIII.

Twas his well-pointed dart
That digg'd these wells, & drest this Vine;
And taught the wounded HEART
The way into these weeping Eyn.
Vain loves avant! bold hands forbear!
The lamb hath dipp't his white foot here.

XVIV.

And now where're he strayes,
Among the Galilean mountaines,
Or more unwellcome wayes,
He's follow'd by two faithfull fountaines;
Two walking baths; two weeping motions;
Portable, & compendious oceans.

XX.

O thou, thy lord's fair store!
In thy so rich & rare expenses,
Even when he show'd most poor,
He might provoke the wealth of Princes.
What Prince's wanton'st pride e're could
Wash with Sylver, wipe with Gold.

XXI.

Who is that King, but he
Who calls't his Crown to be call'd Thine,
That thus can boast to be Waited on by a wandring
        mine,
A voluntary mint, that strowes
Warm sylver shoures where're he goes!

XXII.

O pretious Prodigall!
Fair spend-thrift of thy self; thy measure
    (Mercilesse love!) is all.
    Even to the last Pearle in thy treasure.
All places, Times, & objects be
Thy teare's sweet opportunity.

XXIII.

Does the day-starre rise?
    Still thy starres doe fall & fall
Does day close his eyes?
    Still the FOUNTAIN weeps for all.
Let night or day doe what they will,
Thou hast thy task; thou weepest still.

XXIV.

Does thy song lull the air?
    Thy falling teares keep faith full time.
Does thy sweet-breath'd praire
    Up in clouds of incense climb?
Still at each sigh, that is, each stop,
A bead, that is, A TEAR, does drop.

XXV.

At these thy weeping gates,
    (Watching their watry motion)
Each winged moment waits,
    Takes his TEAR, & gets him gone.
By thine Ey's tinct enobled thus
Time layes him up; he's pretious.

XXVI.

Not, so long she lived,
Shall thy tomb report of thee;
But, so long she greived,
Thus must we date thy memory.
Others by moments, months, & yeares
Measure their ages; thou, by TEARES.

XXVII.

So doe perfumes expire.
So sigh tormented sweets, opprest
With proud unpittying fire.
Such teares the suffring Rose that's vext.
With ungentle flames does shed,
Sweating in a too warm bed.

XXVIII.

Say, ye bright brothers,
The figitive sons of those fair Eyes
Your fruitfull mothers!
What make you here? what hopes can'tice
You to be born! what cause can borrow
You from Those nests of noble sorrow?

XXIX.

Whither away so fast!
For sure the sordid earth
Your Sweetnes cannot tast
Nor does the dust deserve your birth.
Sweet, whither hast you then? o say
Why you trip so fast away?

XXX.

We goe not to seek,
The darlings of Auroras bed,
The rose's modest Cheek
Nor the violet's humble head.
Though the Feild's eyes too WEEPERS be
Because they want such TEARES as we.

XXXI.

Much lesse mean we to trace
The fortune of inferior gemmes,
Preferr'd to some proud face
Or pertch't upon fear'd Diadems.
Crown'd Heads are toyes. We goe to meet
A worthy object, our Lord's FEET.

In the first stanza, the poet announces the subject matter
for meditation—the repentance of the Magdalen; but unlike
most English devotional poets of the period, he introduces
no realistic detail to enable the reader to visualize the Biblical
setting, or even the heroine. Rather, he proposes at once the
points for meditation. One of the most common critical ob-
jections is that readers soon lose all sense (if they ever had it)
of the Magdalen's presence. Of course: "The Weeper" is a
poem about supernatural repentance, not chiefly about a
woman. The beauty or preciousness of the Magdalen's repentance (and thus, by clear implication, that of any sincere
Christian), proposed in the first stanza, is the major motif of
the poem and extends throughout most of the first thirteen
stanzas: stanzas VII and XI are minor digressions. With the
exception of these two, each stanza of the first half of the
poem dwells on the different aspects of the beauty of the
Saint's contrition. The Magdalen's penitence is beautiful or

precious in at least a triple sense: precious for the saint because it has effected the remission of sins; precious, too, in the eyes of her Saviour, for it is a sign of her love for Him; and precious, finally, because elicited by means of God's grace, purchased by Christ's blood. This is no simple concept.

The digressions are logically related to this central idea. For example, Stanza VII focuses on the *intensity* of the heroine's sorrow, one cause of the efficacy of that penitence. Stanza XI emphasizes those effects of her repentance which other stanzas in the first half of the poem do not discuss: spiritual joy, spiritual marriage to Christ; and, most significantly for biographers of Crashaw, an implication that all Christians share in the accumulated merits of this saint. (A Roman Catholic Doctrine although Crashaw was at present still an Anglican: Stanza XI occurs in the earlier edition of Crashaw's poem as well, which comprises only those lines penned before his conversion to Rome.) The Magdalen's wine, now symbolizing supernatural virtues and accumulated merits, is beneficial to all Christians.

But elsewhere in the first half of "The Weeper," the poet dwells upon the three aspects of the preciousness motif outlined earlier in the essay, developing now one, now the other, and often combining them in various ways to achieve different emphases. For instance, Stanza II introduces the Petrarchan imagery, which, spiritually interpreted, recurs throughout the poem. Stanza III, in asserting that the Magdalen's tears are more beautiful than the sunset, the traditional symbol of the death of Christ, Whose blood had to flow to secure her redemption, points to the root cause of all contrition. Stanzas IV and V, describing the notorious sky-climbing river and cherubic breakfast, dramatize the efficacy of the heroine's repentance. Far from being grotesque excrescences or perverse ornaments, they form a predictable part

of the development of the meditative thought. If a Christian
is meditating on supernatural repentance, surely the question of its efficacy is one which would suggest itself.

An analysis of Stanza XII will make Crashaw's Meditative
procedure clearer.

XII.

> When some new bright Guest
> Takes up among the starres a room,
> And Heaven will make a feast,
> Angels with crystall violls come
> And draw from these full eyes of thine
> Their Master's Water: their own Wine.

The main point here is the acceptability of the Saint's repentance to Heaven, the angelic rejoicing over the tears of
the sinners. Crashaw uses traditional Christian symbols whose
limited meaning contributes to the far wider meaning of the
emblematic picture as a whole. Among the images composing
this emblem two are of special significance: water and wine.
The Magdalen's tears are the Master's "Water" for two reasons: they represent her love for Christ; they are elicited by
His grace. But for the angels her tears are "Wine," under-
lining the theme of celestial rejoicing. We also read an obvious reference to Christ's first miracle, at the Marriage Feast
of Cana; the Saint's conversion, too, is miraculous. Now this
thought, in its main outline, has already occurred in Stanzas
IV and V, but Stanza XII adds to the earlier stanzas the notes
of the Magdalen's love and Christ's special grace as causative
agents, and the miraculous nature of the conversion.

The progression of stanzas in "The Weeper," if not logically inevitable, is nevertheless smooth and reasonable,

usually predictable. The stanza above, for instance, is an extension, both imagistically and ideationally, of Stanza XI. The imagistic link is provided by the notion of joy (symbolized by the wine of Stanza XII). We are back suddenly, but certainly not inexplicably or capriciously, to the rejoicing of the angelic choir. Even Stanza VII (which appears digressive in the light of the whole design) flows naturally from the preceding stanza. The central image of Stanza VI is the setting sun, with its sobering reminder of Christ's sacrifice. It is recognition of the price paid for her redemption which leads to the Magdalen's sorrow in Stanza VII. And the "pearls" of the last line in this stanza leads us smoothly, naturally back to the preciousness motif, taken up again by Stanza VII. (To avoid repetition, the discussion of stanzas VIII–X and XIII is being delayed.)

After Stanza XIII the poem takes a new direction, but we must not be surprised if the poet-meditator returns to consider more fully—or in a new context—some aspect of the motif considered in the first half. For instance, Stanza XXII, rejoicing in the glory to God given by the sinner's change of heart, not surprisingly dwells briefly on the beauty of that penitence, in terms highly reminiscent of the earlier stanzas. Stanzas XIV–XVII explore the relationship between repentance and supernatural joy, a topic which de Sales glowingly recommends as profitable for meditation. Stanza XV is especially noteworthy. Here the poet introduces not new thought, but merely repeats the concepts developed in XIV and XV, and suggested previously in XI, this time "to expand the heart," to adore, the poetic analogue to the Salesian "affective prayer." But why should he lay aside the consideration of points at this particular moment? Because he felt so inclined, the best answer in the world, according to St. Francis.

XVI.

> O sweet contests; of woes
> With loves, of teares with smiles disputing!
> O fair, & Freindly Foes,
> Each other kissing & confuting!
> While rain & Sunshine, Cheeks & Eyes
> Close in kind contrarietyes.

The student of Crashaw's rhetoric will observe how the poet has chosen those images most capable of being set in "contrarities" to move the reader through an unprecedented cross-fire of paradoxes, while the apostrophes which began with the preceding stanza insist with their throb that at this point the poem is undergoing some crisis. Various effects of sound confirm this: alliteration of opposites in 3rd, 4th and final lines; enjambment "of woes/ With loves"; the rhyme "disputing/confuting"; the intensifying cramming of opposites and zeugma into each line of verse, until the penultimate line manages *two* pairs. Crashaw's "rhapsodical moments" owe much more to rhetoric than many of his critics (Joan Bennett, for instance) care to recognize.

Not surprisingly, Stanza XVIII underscores the role of the divine agent in this miraculous conversion, and the next four stanzas (XIX–XXII), reasonably enough, rejoice in the glory given to God by the sinner's change of heart. One reason that this conversion gives glory to God is that to a significant degree it is *voluntary*. In stanza XXI, which clearly goes out of its way to call the heroine a "voluntary mint," the poet aligns himself with the Molinistic (anti-Augustinian) view of Justification. Stanzas XXIII–XXVI broaden the significance of the Saint's conversion to involve all Christians, a point first implied in Stanza XI. Stanza XXIII contains another clear reference to the Treasure House of Grace Theory ("The FOUNTAIN weeps for all"; weeping is the Saint's "task"), and Stanza XXV strikingly reverses the mutability theme: Time stores up the tears of the Saint for the profit of future generations. Stanza XXVI introduces the last point of the meditation—from the point of view of pastoral theology probably the most important thing to say about conversion to righteousness—that the spiritually significant life of the sinner begins only with his conversion, a favorite thought of St. Francis de Sales.

The masterful stanza XXVII, which comprises the end of the meditation proper (and which, in fact, concludes the poem in the first edition), neatly summarizes all the major points of the verse meditation: the great value and beauty of penitence, the ineffable love of the convert for Christ, the acute pain resulting from recognition of past sins and personal inadequacy. All this is expressed symbolically; or emblematically, for the four images of the stanza, which comprise a unified picture, have exactly the same logical interrelationship as the concepts they embody: the Magdalen (rose) consumed by love for Christ (flame) and sorrowing, as a result, over past sin (tears) gives up the spirit, which ascends to Christ with a sweet odor (perfume). The reader will recall that after the formal conclusion of a Salesian meditation (usually a summary of the main points) the meditator must make a brief application to his own life by drawing from the meditation some short lesson to which he will return later in the day. The last four lines of "The Weeper" comprise the "spiritual nosegay" or coda: we must renounce all earthly joys in favor of Christ's love. This thought is the only proper ending for meditations on sin and repentance, according to de Sales. In the last four stanzas the lovely images of the first half of the poem pass in review and are rejected; for in the final analysis "The Weeper" rejects the world of the senses, calmly but unequivocally.

A prose paraphrase of the poem should reveal its structure clearly. Sorrow over sin such as Mary Magdalen's is beautiful and precious (I–XIII), intimately and paradoxically linked with joy (XIV–XVII). In this experience God plays a key role and rejoices over the glory which it gives Him (XVIII–XXII). But Christians ought to rejoice over this conversion, too, for they stand to profit from it (XXIII–XXV) and they must remind themselves that they have not begun to live, spiritually, until they have experienced a change of heart similar to the Saint's (XXVI). The lesson to be drawn from this meditation is that we must renounce all earthly joys in favor of Christ's love (last four stanzas). The progression of thought, although not inevitable, is certainly a firm, logical association of ideas.

The controlling, meditative purpose of "The Weeper" has influenced not only the formal design of the poem but its imagery as well. Critics such as Wallerstein, Warren, and Williams have pointed out that Crashaw's imagery is typically symbolical and that the poet not infrequently packs away a good deal of intellectual content into his conceits (though a surprisingly large number of recent critics do not concede any of this). But these intellectual conceits occur in poems or in passages which develop a concept in a straightforward, logical, relatively terse manner. Far less admired are those passages in which Crashaw seems merely to repeat the same concept over and over in different images, a habit usually attributed to the Baroque love for dramatic emphasis and luxurious amplitude. Less generous critics simply write it off as redundancy of the worst sort. Now the Baroque asthetic is obviously at work here, but Crashaw's imagery is hardly ever truly redundant or even *merely* iterative for purposes of dramatic emphasis. The embodying of the same *basic* concept in a series of increasingly lush images usually represents a steady, subtle, but quite significant development of thought. When Crashaw repeats, it is with a significant difference. Insufficient experience with the emblem tradition, and with emblem reading, in which Crashaw and his readers were steeped, is perhaps accountable for this almost universal misinterpretation of the "iterative" images.

To illustrate the Baroque love for dramatic emphasis and redundant magniloquence, critics usually turn to "The Weeper," especially to its first stanza. Of all the critics of "The Weeper," Stephen Manning seems the most generous, but even he sees in the first stanza merely an "accumulation of images," whose justification, allegedly, is that the poet wishes to express his sense of inadequacy to express divine truths.[2] No doubt, but the crucial point is that, although Crashaw has embodied the same *basic* concept in different images, for emphasis, he has also subtly but significantly modified the thought with each embellishment. In his typically direct jubilant manner, Crashaw proposes the subject for meditation, the repentance of the Magdalen, represented by her weeping, symbolized, in turn, by the springs of water (from her two eyes). He develops the image: the springs give rise to "Silver-footed rills," because the Saint's repentance is beautiful and precious (silver) in the sight of her Saviour, "silver" pointing, also, to the purifying power of the tears (contrition). The icon has been rendered esthetically pleasing because its conceptual analogue is beautiful. The two responses—the esthetic and conceptual—are in co-articulation. The springs' giving rise to rills suggests, furthermore, the magnitude of the Magdalen's sorrow. This imagistic turn, then, points to several important concepts, as does the next line ("Ever bubbling things") with its reminder that the Magdalen's tears flow unceasingly, for she grieves continually. Some measure of sorrow for sin should always be with us.

The "thawing crystal" suggests the miraculous nature of our heroine's conversion. According to Sir Thomas Browne (*Pseudodoxia Epidemica* I, i) crystal is "ice or snow concreted, and by duration of time, congealed beyond liquidation." And the crystal, hard and cold, also points to the depths of depravity into which Mary Magdalen had fallen, for the Bible typically uses hardness of heart as a symbol of wickedness or perversity. The imagery was perhaps suggested by an emblem entitled "Cordis Emollitio" (The Softening of the Heart) in *Schola Cordis,* in which conversion to righteousness is represented by Anima's frozen heart melting rapidly as the sunny rays from the eyes and halo of Christ (Divine Love) reach it.[3] The melting hills of snow also suggest her conversion from sin; but snow, the traditional symbol of chastity, points to the purity of heart to which the Saint now aspires, and "Still spending, never spent!" calls attention once again to the permanence of the Magdalen's repentance. The paradox is intended to arouse our wonder, to encourage further meditation. Finally, the poet states explicitly the subject of meditation: "I mean/Thy fair eyes, sweet Magdalene!" But even the fair eyes are merely symbols of the Saint's contrition. The Petrarchan tradition is partly responsible for Crashaw's focusing on eye imagery. The divine romance motif is subtly suggested, even in this first stanza. Interestingly, in spite of the elaboration, a prose rendering of this allegedly redundant stanza requires more than twice as many words. Every bit of ornamentation, from the "silver-footed rills" to the "snowy hills" expresses a rather clearly determinable conceptual meaning.

Other passages sometimes cited as examples of Baroque redundancy are Stanzas VIII, IX, X and XIII. These stanzas have a special unity; all develop the preciousness motif. Stanza VIII compares the loveliest objects which the material world offers to the tears of our heroine, and finds them very much wanting. All this is to emphasize the preciousness of supernatural repentance. The *prosopopeia* (the attributing of human emotions to subhuman objects) which is so liberally sprinkled throughout these stanzas was regarded, in the Renaissance, as an effective means of emotional heightening. Thus the dewdrop (with symbolical suggestions of grace and the Resurrection) would rather be a tear. The poet has surely gone out of his way to enhance the loveliness of the material object, but in order to emphasize a concept. So, the tears of Mary Magdalen are more beautiful than dewdrops; but if this comparison is to be really telling, the latter must be endowed with all possible beauty. Also envying the loveliness of the tears are the lily and the primrose, each introducing new symbolical overtones: the lily is a traditional symbol of chastity, and the primrose (because of its white color) suggests innocence.

Stanza X compares the tears of the Saint to still another natural object. But this is repetition with a real difference. The *beauty* of the repentance was stressed in Stanza VIII; now, in Stanza X, the marvelous *effects* are celebrated. Balsam may have curative effects on the body, but contrition razes out the cancerous tissues of sin. In Stanza X both the dew and the balsam ("drops") once again lament their inferiority. Things natural and material melt into insignificance when compared to things spiritual.

Stanza XIII returns once again to the superiority of our heroine's tears, this time to celebrate their superiority not over the world of nature but over the sphere of secular concerns. The Golden Tagus was a familiar symbol of earthly, secular values (especially those of the business world).

Boethius makes use of the symbol (*De Cons. III*) as does Skelton in "Phillip Sparrow" (875–876). But this golden river envies our Saint's "silver streams." Silver is more precious than gold: the value system of shallow earthlings is overthrown.

Probably the most notorious passage in Baroque poetry is the sky-climbing river of tears and the cream-sipping cherub of Stanzas IV and V. As was pointed out earlier, the concept of beauty of contrition leads, sooner or later, to a consideration of its efficacy. Stanza IV symbolizes this acceptability to God by causing the tears to ascend heavenwards. Mr. Alvarez, who grants the symbolical nature of the imagery, nevertheless finds these lines grotesque because an idea "has been pushed to an extreme: that because the weeping of the Magdalen was pious, it must have reached heaven." [4] He complains also that here, as elsewhere in Crashaw, it is possible to see *how* a given image has arrived, but not *why*. On the contrary, no image has been pushed to an extreme. That the tears of repentant sinner should be acceptable to Heaven is traditional Catholic and Anglican dogma. And what could be more natural than that in the course of a meditation on contrition, the efficacy of such sorrow should suggest itself quite early to the meditator? No one fairly well acquainted with the Baroque poetic method or emblem literature can be surprised that the poet's way of expressing this concept (acceptability of contrition) is to arrange for the symbol of sorrow to flow upwards; especially since the poet has carefully prepared for this imagistic turn, with the "falling" imagery of preceding stanzas. The falling stars, mere material objects, however beautiful, deservedly fall to the ground. The natural and materials falls as the divine rises—thoroughly conventional, even predictable. And if basic physical laws are violated, so much the better: such a conversion is in itself miraculous.

The sky-climbing river of tears has merged with the milky way (traditionally, the highway to heaven, as in George Herbert's "Prayer"), but the tears of the Magdalen, immeasurably more precious than these stars, is the cream which rises above them. The physical property of cream (which causes it to rise above milk) and its symbolic value (suggesting preciousness, as in many popular expressions) have been used as analogues to express spiritual truth. Perhaps the proverbial land flowing with milk and honey, used in the Old Testament as a type of Heaven, suggested this imagistic development. The last two lines of Stanza IV (raised perhaps by Psalm 148.4): how could waters exist in the heavens, whose nature is fire? But such astronomical controversies, Crashaw implies, are insignificant when compared to this spiritual truth: the tears of the contrite sinner *do* reach Heaven.

Not only God but even the angelic host is jubilant. The Cherubic breakfast in Stanza V signifies the rejoicing of the angels over the spiritual triumph which these tears represent. The piling up of gastronomic detail seems intended to express the intensity of angelic joy and thus, by implication, the preciousness and efficacy of sincere contrition. Surely it is not oversubtle to suggest that these two stanzas comprise a highly embellished emblem of this theme: "There shall be more rejoicing in Heaven over one converted sinner than over ten just men." (Luke 15:7) The cherub finds the tears (repentance) sweet, which in the earlier seventeenth century more often meant refreshing, agreeable, dearly loved. The phrase "addes sweetnes to his sweetest lippes"—one of the most maligned in the poem—refers to the dogma of the Treasure House of Grace, the belief that all members of

Christ's Mystical Body (all united to Him by grace) share in the merits of the saints. The scholastic theologians (and some Anglicans such as Hooker) defined grace not as a mere *relationship* between God and man but as an actual *quality* inhering in the soul, which makes it agreeable, pleasing unto God. Like any other quality, such as warmth, grace exists in varying degrees of intensity. Thus, the cherub, already in the state of grace, finds himself spiritually enhanced by an intensification of grace. Far from merely forcing the idea of cloying sweetness on the reader, this maligned line introduces one of the most invigoratingly controversial dogmas of the seventeenth century.

Our chief concern however, has not been to defend these lines esthetically but to insist that each embellishment of these peculiar (to us) images is firmly grounded in thought. It is just as easy to see *why* as *how* each image arrives. Image glides into image just as the controlling, meditative thought demands. "The Weeper" has been studied as a Baroque verse meditation in the Salesian mode.[5] Crashaw embodies the "points" of the meditation in lush symbolical images, which, like rhetorical devices such as paradox and prosopopeia, are chiefly devotional in aim: they seek to arouse wonder, to tempt the reader, by their beauty and wit, to dwell on the thought. As elsewhere in his religious lyrics, Crashaw eschews the personal, specific element. He does not, typically, attempt to objectify a particular moment of religious experience. Rather, the verse meditation is objective, as if the poet were composing a meditation for Everyman.

NOTES

[1] Leland Chambers' fine article: "In Defense of 'The Weeper,' " *PLL* 3: 111–21. Covers quite different ground from my explication herein.

[2] Manning, p. 37.

[3] Benedictus van Haeften, *Schola Cordia* (Antwerp, 1629). See the German translation, *Hertzen Schuel* (Augsburg, 1664), p. 253. Quarles reproduced this emblem (1635). See Francis Quarles, *Emblems, Divine and Moral*, ed. William Tegg (London, 1866), p. 285.

[4] A. Alvarez, *The School of Donne* (London, 1961), pp. 99–100.

[5] Much of what this chapter has said about Crashaw applies to many Puritan poets. A study of Perry Miller's anthology of New England Puritan poets reveals startling similarities. The Puritans need to be restudied in relationship to the Baroque.

CONCLUSION

Believing that many critics, even recent ones, have erred gravely in their assessments and interpretations chiefly because of their failure fully to appreciate the intellectual element in Crashaw's imagery and his architectonic power, we have tried to demonstrate that Crashaw's imagery is almost always purely symbolic. The characteristic Crashaw image is not intended to be visualized vividly; the reader is expected, rather, to dwell on the concept embodied therein. Even those imagistic developments usually labeled grotesque are firmly grounded in thought. Crashaw's emblematic images fall into two categories: the *contracted* emblem, a single image into which several related thoughts have been tightly packed; and the *extended* emblem, characterized by a lavish, leisurely imagistic embellishment which is not redundant—as Crashaw's critics have maintained—but which subtly, yet significantly, advances the developing thought. The most eloquent testimony to the intellectual side of Crashaw's genius is his practice of using traditional Christian symbols as building blocks for emblematic pictures of his own devising.

Emblem books, one must keep ever in mind, were enormously popular in Crashaw's England. Crashaw is at times indebted to specific emblem plates, but it was the emblematic mode of utterance, even more than individual emblem plates, that affected his poetic, by enabling him to devise verbal emblems to embody devotional thought. In these latter images, which cannot be traced to a specific source in an emblem book, the pattern of the emblem is nonetheless clearly discernible. The image is characterized by a peculiar, often gross, unmistakable visual and tactile vividness; and there is a dwelling on concrete detail, on sensuous particulars, which are directly related to clear concepts of a theological or moral character. The seventeenth-century emblematist, typically, represented a Biblical proverbial metaphor graphically and literally, connecting each sensuous particular with a concept. Crashaw does exactly this. We are dealing with a clearly traceable circuit: from Biblical or proverbial metaphor into graphic representation and then back again into poetic metaphor. This, briefly, is the probable history of many of Crashaw's images.

This book has proposed, furthermore, that readers who label Crashaw exotic, alien, feminine, or psychotic are unaware that the Baroque was not a specifically Roman Catholic movement but very much "in the air" even in Protestant countries. In England the Baroque was far more openly manifested in the highly popular second- and third-rate literature than in the products of the aristocratic belletristic tradition. The Baroque especially affected certain segments of seventeenth-century English Puritans, particularly those far left of center (Godwin, Sterry, Rous, for instance). Rous, the Independent, eminent member of the Barebones Parliament, is more exuberant than Crashaw, considerably bolder in his appropriation and development of sensuous, erotic imagery from the Song of Songs. Not even the most rabid Papist-haters hesitated to

use Catholic devotional writings, which exerted an immense
—indeed, a major—influence on English Protestant spirituality. Crashaw is in no sense foreign; rather, he dipped into
native English wells which other major poets of his day
eschewed. For this reason critics have been unable to place
him securely in the mainstream of English literature.

Keeping in mind the openness of the religious climate, one
need not be surprised that St. Francis de Sales exerted a major
influence on Crashaw—on his spiritual formation and on the
structure of his religious lyrics. St. Francis is responsible for
that suave detachment and objectivity which characterize
even Crashaw's most rhapsodic moments, for the startling
absence of so many favorite topics of seventeenth-century
spirituality—hell, death, sin; and for his celebration of spiritual heroines who surrender their wills completely to the
Divine Spouse. Especially influential was the Salesian method
of meditation, which forms the substructure of many religious lyrics. Unlike its Ignatian predecessor, the Salesian
method does not stress composition of place, application of
the senses, introspection, or the arousing of violent emotions.
In fact, it rules out the last two. The Salesian method encourages, instead, a calm, leisurely reflection on various
"points" (concepts) in as spiritual a manner as possible, to
raise the heart up to God in "affective prayer," the poetic
analogue of which is the rhapsodic flight. Crashaw is a poet-
meditator of the Salesian school.

"The Weeper" has been studied as a baroque verse meditation. Here, as usual, Crashaw eschews the personal, specific
element. The meditation is objective, as if the poet were
composing a meditation for Everyman. The devotional
thoughts or points of meditation are embodied in lush emblems, which, like rhetorical devices such as paradox and
prosopopeia, are chiefly devotional in aim: they are intended

to arouse wonder—to tempt the reader, by their beauty and wit, to contemplate the thought. In short, this is the baroque way of avoiding a stock response to theological commonplace.

The subject of "The Weeper" is the repentance of Mary Magdalen, chiefly a symbol of the contrite Christian. The poem, consisting of a series of logically related points, usually expressed emblematically, is organized on a Salesian model, a substructure evident in many of Crashaw's religious lyrics. "The Weeper" considers contrition from several points of view: the leading motifs (often reiterated, as the Salesian method of meditation encourages) are the value and efficacy of contrition. The concluding four stanzas are the poetic application of a Salesian contribution to the history of formal meditation, the "Spiritual nosegay."

This study has sought to readjust the popular image of Crashaw, to prove that his control is typically firm, that he is not so completely absorbed in emotions and sensuous embellishments that he fails to think. Indeed, when Crashaw *does* fail, the lapse is usually due to his preoccupation with concept at the expense of image. But even those rhapsodic passages, for which he is universally admired, owe much of their effectiveness to the architectonic power of his thought.

APPENDIX I

*Crashaw Scholarship in the Twentieth Century
Survey and Assessment*

For reasons which Austin Warren makes clear, critical opinion
of Crashaw during the eighteenth and nineteenth centuries
was far from favorable. Even Sir Edmund Gosse in *Seventeenth Century Studies* does little but reinforce misapprehensions. Between the date of the second edition of Sir Edmund
Gosse's *Seventeenth Century Studies* (1885) and the end of
the First World War there extends a period characterized
by an almost complete neglect of Crashaw.

Nevertheless, within this period, J. R. Tutin's edition of
Crashaw (1905) deserves mention as the first in this century.
Yet one wonders what motivated this editor; for Crashaw
has never been more unkindly handled than by the gentleman
chosen to write the introduction to this edition, Canon Beeching. Horrified by the "indecorous" use of the imagery of
the "Song of Songs," he assures us that the temper not only
of the English race but even of the language itself "stands
opposed to the soul's religious rapture."

Courthope, too, deserves mention, for the third volume of his *History of English Literature* (1905) treats Crashaw in much more detail than was then customary. To Gosse's religious analysis, Courthope adds only the observation that no poet has depended so exclusively on amorous imagery and on "allusions which inspire the genius of the Pagan muse." Although a literary historian, Courthope knows next to nothing, obviously, about the Christian mystical tradition. Even such a noted study as Sir Herbert Grierson's *English Literature During the First Half of the Seventeenth Century* (1906) contributes surprisingly little. Grierson reminds us that Crashaw's conceits are different from Donne's ("after the confectionery manner of the Italians"). He goes out of his way to find reasons to admire Crashaw, but admires him, one fears, for the wrong reasons. Crashaw's lyrics are supposedly characterized, at their best, by the two supreme qualities of great lyric poetry, ardor and music; and our poet is compared to Shelley and Swinburne—equivocal praise, at best. Thus, obviously, in the matter of Crashaw scholarship the first two decades of this century can be described as a spillover of later nineteenth-century thought.

The next significant publication to discuss Crashaw appeared in 1919—P. H. Osmond's *The Mystical Poets of the English Church*—a study perhaps unparalleled for its vehement denunciations and gross misapprehensions: Osmond completely fails to understand the Baroque spirit or the emblem. Also appearing in 1919 (*Contemporary Review*) is an article by Constance Spender—"Richard Crashaw, 1613–1648," a brief biographical study refreshingly free of aspersions.

Crashaw scholarship enjoys a sudden upsurge in the first half of the twenties, with Burton Confrey's "A Note on Richard Crashaw" (*Church Quarterly Review*, 1923), Cyril

Falls' "The Divine Poet" (*The Nineteenth Century*, 1923),
K. M. Loudon's *Two Mystic Poets & Other Essays* (1923),
Lord Chalmers' "Richard Crashaw: Poet and Saint" (*In Memoriam Adolphus Ward, Master of Peterhouse*), and Alexander Pulling's "Crashaw the Poet: His Pedigree" (*N & Q*,
1925). One regrets making short shrift of these pioneers of
the early twenties, for they stimulated interest in Crashaw;
yet their scholarly contributions, viewed objectively, are
meagre, perhaps because they did not understand the Baroque.
Moreover, they had little knowledge of either the emblem
tradition or the Christian mystical tradition, and seem to have
had peculiar difficulties in setting Crashaw in his proper intellectual and historical milieu.

The year 1925 marks the publication of Mario Praz' monumental and justly celebrated *Secentismo e Marinismo in
Inghilterra: John Donne e Richard Crashaw*. To Signor Praz
we owe the expression"spiritualizzamento del sense" (spiritualization of the senses), a phrase which aptly describes the
major educational and esthetic movement of the early seventeenth century. The author brilliantly describes the type of
imagery developed to serve this purpose, and demonstrates
how this imagery could mean almost all things to all men—
mere literary fashion for one, sincere expression of mystical
fervor for another. Signor Praz also calls attention (especially in his discussion of Marino's influence) to the international character of seventeenth-century esthetic movements.

But the reader who expects empathy for Crashaw from an
Italian critic will be surprised and disappointed to hear Praz
describe Crashaw's spirit as feminine and morbidly sensuous,
and complain that the "spiritualizzamento del sense" is rarely
realized.

Kathleen Lea's frequently quoted article "Conceits"
(*MLR*, 1925) is one of the first studies to insist upon the

conceptual nature of seventeenth-century imagery. Warning us not to visualize Crashaw's images too vividly, she calls attention to their symbolic nature. (Failure to make this emphasis is perhaps the chief weakness of Signor Praz' otherwise excellent study.) The development of Miss Lea's thesis has formed a significant part of the fruitful studies of Wallerstein and White. R. L. Megroz' "Crashaw and Thompson" (in *Francis Thompson: The Poet of Earth in Heaven*, 1927) serves to remind us how far from the Baroque esthetic nineteenth-century Catholicism had developed. T. S. Eliot, who has done so much to popularize metaphysical poetry in general (Donne in particular), has not served Crashaw particularly well. He recognizes, for example, the intellectual element in Crashaw's poetry (and such recognition is in itself a welcome change) but finds Crashaw's intellectuality "perverse" (*For Lancelot Andrewes*, 1928, p. 124).

These critical studies of the twenties were perhaps one of the stimuli which prompted Martin's famous edition of Crashaw's poems in 1927. On the continent of Europe, too, the late twenties saw a sudden upsurge of interest in Baroque literature. First in a distinguished line of German critics of Crashaw and English Baroque poetry is Wilhelm Tholen ("Ein Englischer Dichter and Mystiker der Barochzeit," *Das neue Ufer*, 1927). Regrettably, this perceptive critic is not strong on Christian symbolism.

The thirties opened with the important contribution to seventeenth-century scholarship of George Williamson. In *The Donne Tradition* (1930) Mr. Williamson tries valiantly to establish a direct connection between Crashaw and the Donnean school. He is obviously hard pressed, his difficulty arising necessarily, given his view of Crashaw's imagery. The emblem, not the conceit, is what serves to tie Crashaw's poetic method to Donne's. But the emblematic element is exactly what Williamson underplays.

The year 1932 saw the publication of W. P. Friederich's
*Spiritualismus und Sensualismus in der Englischen Barock-
lyrik,* which expands several theses first proposed by Praz.
According to Friederich the inner unity of the sixteenth century ("innere einheit des 16. jahrhundert") was shattered
by a warlike clash between Christian asceticism and the
worldly, fleshly demands of the Pagan Renaissance. The tension resulting from this conflict is the essential spirit of the
Baroque and pervades the English Baroque lyrics (particularly those of Crashaw). Friederick Wild's "Zur problem des
Barocks in der Englischen Dichtung" (*Halle,* 1934 and
Anglia, 1935) focuses sharply on Crashaw as representative of
the Baroque in English Poetry but adds little to Praz' study.

T. O. Beachcroft developed briefly several portions of
Miss Lea's thesis ("Crashaw and The Baroque Style," *Criterion,* XIII, April, 1934, 407–425). Erroneously, he views Crashaw's chief enemy "as Protestant aggression." Joan Bennett's
Four Metaphysical Poets (1934), while it deserves high praise
for its analysis of Donne is disappointing in its approach to
Crashaw. Mrs. Bennett errs chiefly because she does not perceive the emblematic (and typically quite traditional) element in Crashaw's imagery. Regrettably, this brilliant critic
does little more than set forth in modern dress the reactions of
such older critics as Osmond and Gosse; she laments, in essential fact, the paucity of that very element in his imagery
which some later studies have focused upon. For Crashaw
scholarship, Mrs. Bennett's popular book must be accounted a
step backward.

Elbridge Colby's rather skimpy but interesting treatment
of Crashaw's Catholicism in *English Catholic Poets, Chaucer
to Dryden* (1936) is more worthy of note than Francis E.
Barker's study of Andrewes' influence on Crashaw, with its
weakly supported conclusions (*TLS,* 1937). E. I. Watkin,
in his "Richard Crashaw," in *The English Way: Studies in*

English Sanctity (1933) lay the grounds for his more recent publication, *Poets and Mystics* (1953). Even in his work of 1933 E. I. Watkin was aware (more so than Praz) that the devotional practices which influenced Crashaw's religious lyrics were not limited to the Catholic continent but were actually very much "in the air" even in England.

During the middle and late thirties appeared the important studies of Wallerstein, White, and Warren. These three studies, since they have established the main directions which Crashaw criticism should take, and since they have linked the correct interpretation and appreciation of Crashaw's poetry to the emblem and to the Baroque, deserve to be classified as milestones. Because of them, one is tempted to call the thirties the "Golden Age" of Crashaw scholarship.

The first of these studies, Miss Wallerstein's *Richard Crashaw, A Study in Style and Poetic Development* (1935), traces for the first time the development of Crashaw's poetic style. She sees in the mature style a superimposition of the ingenuity of neo-Latin epigrammatists and the sophistication of Marino on the sensuous richness inherited from the Spenserian tradition. But a more significant contribution is Miss Wallerstein's emphasis on the intellectual element in his imagery, on his use of sensuous objects to express pure abstractions, a method derived from the emblem tradition. However, one might suggest respectfully that Miss Wallerstein has written off the problem of Crashaw's stylistic development rather too easily. Many other influences were at work —the meditative traditions, to name a particularly important one. No book treating Crashaw has been so widely quoted— nor so widely ignored.

A year after the publication of Miss Wallerstein's important study, Helen C. White's *The Metaphysical Poets* illustrated how each of the major metaphysical poets pursued a personal quest for truth, and related the expression of their religious thought to the theological and intellectual milieu of the earlier seventeenth century. The two chapters devoted to Crashaw discuss the nature of Crashaw's religious experience, stressing the intellectual element in his imagery and making the important point, for the first time in scholarly literature, that the structure of the Crashaw lyric is typically firm and clear.

In 1939 Austin Warren published his *Richard Crashaw, A Study in Baroque Sensibility*. Warren's description of Baroque sensibility has been accepted too uncritically. In demonstrating clearly the relationship of the Baroque to the emblem and the Counter-Reformation, Warren dangerously exaggerates the link between the sensual aspects of the Baroque and Roman Catholicism and fails fully to appreciate the intellectual base of Baroque sensuousness and ornamentation. Warren's viewpoint on these sensual elements makes it difficult for him to do full justice to the intellectual side of Crashaw or to place him in the mainstream of English literature. In spite of this limitation, Warren's brilliant discussion of Crashaw's symbolism merits high praise as one of the most significant contributions to Crashaw scholarship. All subsequent studies of Crashaw's symbolism have used Warren's study as a springboard.

After the highly productive period of the late thirties there is a lull of at least a decade; for the output of the forties, judged as a whole, pales into mediocrity when compared with that of either the thirties or late fifties. Robert Sharp's *From Donne to Dryden, the Revolt Against Metaphysical Poetry* (1940) has nothing new to say about Crashaw; the critic misses an opportunity to show how Crashaw, in his nonemblematic passages (and there are many) is in a direct line which originates with Jonson; and, more important, how

Crashaw made some significant contributions of his own to "neoclassical" verse. It was not for nothing that Pope found much to admire in Crashaw's "numbers." Crashaw, as usual, is viewed as a dead-end.

Sackville-West's interesting study *The Eagle and the Dove* (1943), Miriam Bernard's "More than Woman" (*Catholic World*, 1943) and Michael Moloney's article "Richard Crashaw" (*Catholic World*, 1945) represent the only work done on Crashaw during World War II. This third study deserves far more attention than it has received. The late Mr. Moloney makes two important observations ignored by subsequent critics. The critic points out (although with insufficient illustration) that Crashaw's luxuriance is not one of line and image (as it is with Spenser) but of image alone; the verse remains restrained. Mr. Moloney then makes the interesting point that Crashaw's true master is Jonson, an overstatement surely, but perhaps a useful one. Critics from Coleridge to Wallerstein have customarily linked Crashaw quite glibly with Elizabethan "sweetness." Actually, as Moloney points out, Crashaw rather typically eschews the sweetness characteristic of Elizabethan sentiment. These two points are fertile ground for seventeenth-century scholarship, especially the first thesis of Mr. Moloney's, that involving the distinction between the Baroque and Spenserian luxuriance. No critic has yet succeeded in drawing a line sharp enough to be functional between Spenserian pictorial fluidity or luxuriance and Baroque ornamentation. The problem is a formidable one.

In *The Fantasticks* (1945) W. S. Scott gives a psychological explanation for the "excesses" of Crashaw's religious lyrics, an explanation which has become, unfortunately, standard. Crashaw, allegedly, diverted to his religious verse all warmth and emotional feelings which would otherwise have shown themselves in more "normal" ways. Thus his meditative lyrics are supposedly touched by "strong animalism," his poetry clearly showing the dual effect of a strongly inhibited character and a somewhat sensual religion. For Mr. Scott (as for many subsequent critics) "Name Above Every Name" becomes the *locus classicus* for Crashaw abnormalities, a veritable storehouse of thinly disguised perversions.

The tercentenary commemoration of Crashaw's first book of English verse (in 1946) was the occasion for a brief anonymous article of little significance appearing in *TLS* (June 1), entitled "Richard Crashaw, Poet and Saint." In the same year appeared W. L. Doughty's *Studies in Religious Poetry of the Seventeenth Century*. The one weak chapter is that which treats Crashaw. Mr. Doughty takes great pains to do justice to our poet, but fails; for he understands neither the meditative purpose of Crashaw's lyrics nor the method employed to achieve it. The writer complains, for instance, that the physical aspects of the Crucifixion exercise a morbid fascination for Crashaw whereas it is precisely the *physical* aspects which our poet ignores.

Anthony F. Allison is a critic whose contributions deserve more than passing notice. His two articles, published in 1947, "St. Theresa and Sensuous Language" (*RES*) and "Some Influences in Crashaw's Poem 'On a Prayer Booke sent to Mrs. M. R.'" (*RES*) are richly suggestive. The first of these especially is remarkable for its sane approach to the use of erotic language in religious literature. Subsequent critics have ignored this brief study at their own peril. In 1948 the same critic published (in *RES*) "Crashaw and St. François de Sales," a study needing expansion. In this article Mr. Allison calls attention to the influence of Salesian religious attitudes, not the much more important matter of Salesian methods of meditation. Almost all other critics who have bothered to consider historical influences have pointed, very misleadingly, to St. Ignatius of Loyola's *Spiritual Exercises*.

There is hardly space here to do justice to William Empson's controversial *Seven Types of Ambiguity* (1947), a classical example of the new criticism which insists on looking *only* at the poem itself. Suffice it to say that no poet has suffered more than Crashaw from a wilful ignoring of historical background. In the same year the Rev. Walter J. Ong, S. J., published an article highly relevant (although indirectly) to much seventeenth-century religious poetry, especially to that of Crashaw. "Wit and Mystery: A Revaluation in Medieval Latin Hymnody" (*Speculum*) does much to show that "wit" and the Christian religion are not only compatible but, indeed, mutually supporting.

The year 1948 was an unusually productive one. One of the most valuable contributions of the decade is Kerby Neill's "Structure and Symbol in Crashaw's 'Hymn in the Nativity' " (*PMLA*, 1948). Mr. Neill demonstrates how Crashaw in his revision of this poem, made the structural pattern much clearer by substituting structural symbols for mere sense images, by emending a few lines, by dropping and adding others. Mr. Neill stresses Crashaw's *conceptual unity*, a crucial matter ignored by critics since Miss White. The critic makes admirable use of his knowledge of Christian symbolism in his detailed analysis, the first really extended analysis of a Crashaw poem based upon a true understanding of the symbolic nature of the imagery. Itrat-Husain (*The Mystical Element in the Metaphysical Poets of the 17th Century*, 1948) is rather well aware of the aims of the Baroque religious poet and seeks to absolve Crashaw of the charges of meaningless extravagance. The rapturous soaring qualities of the lyrics, he points out, are expressions of the state of mystical life, not merely literary devices. But since he fails to stress the intellectual side of Crashaw, his efforts are not always fruitful. Mr. Itrat-Husain tends to exaggerate the influence on Crashaw of the *Spiritual Exercises* of St. Ignatius, but his treatment of St. Teresa's influence is valuable and well supported. Also published in 1948 were two very short but careful studies by George W. Williams: "Crashaw's 'Letter to the Countess of Denbigh' " (*Explicator*, VI), "Textual Revision in Crashaw's 'Upon the Bleeding Crucifix,' " (*Papers of the Bibliographical Society of Virginia*). This second study shows how fully conscious Crashaw himself was of the emblematic symbolic nature of his imagery.

The decade comes to an end with the publication of three short articles: Mario Praz' "Drummond and Crashaw" (*TLS*); Martin Turnell's "Richard Crashaw after 300 Years" (*The Nineteenth Century*), an assessment of Crashaw's contemporary reputation; and Basil Willey's "Richard Crashaw," a memorial lecture delivered at Peterhouse (1949). In general, one can assert that scholarly literature treating Crashaw in the forties is characterized by mediocrity and by a strange lack of continuity with the great studies of the thirties. Neill, Moloney, and Allison are the critics who significantly advanced Crashavian scholarship during this decade.

The fifties show us a much brighter picture. 1950 saw the publication of C. R. Cammell's "The Divine Poet: Richard Crashaw" (N & E Review), followed by L. C. Martin's "An Uncredited Crashaw Manuscript" (*TLS*, 1952). John Peter's "Crashaw and 'The Weeper' " (*Scrutiny*, 1953) is the second detailed literary analysis of a Crashaw poem, Niell's being the first. Mr. Peter's contribution reminds readers (as several other critics had done before him) that they should not attempt to visualize the images, that they are not present for their value as picture or sensation. Unfortunately, he does *not* go on to say that the images stand for clear concepts. Mr. Peter maintains instead that their purpose is to establish mood or "tone"; that is, at best, a quite secondary purpose. Inevitably, Mr. Peter's assumption concerning the *essential* purpose of the imagery does not lead to a particularly flattering evaluation of the poem's esthetic merits.

Even less inclined to flatter Crashaw is Odette de Mourgues, the least sympathetic of Crashaw's contemporary critics. Her book *Metaphysical, Baroque and Précieux Poetry* has the laudable purpose of making clear-cut distinctions among these three terms, for both English and French poetry. Miss de Mourgues' greater contribution is surely to French poetry. She sees the Baroque as providing an essentially "distorted" vision of life, as pandering, in the name of religion, to the baser emotions. She finds it impossible to praise even "On the Wounds of Our Crucified Savior"; here also she finds perversities. The misapprehensions of the late nineteenth century critics have returned.

In recent years Crashaw scholarship has returned to pick up an idea which Miss White first suggested in her book *The Metaphysical Poets*—the meditative nature (in a formal sense) of Crashaw's religious lyrics. Louis Martz' *The Poetry of Meditation* (1954) has played the key role in this revival of interest in the meditative aspect of the religious lyrics. Martz sees a meditative tradition as the normal central tendency of religious life in Crashaw's time; even Donne's originality is a part of this whole. Formal meditation, Martz shows, came to be regarded as an exercise essential even for the ordinary conduct of the good life. His distinctions between the Ignatian and Salesian methods of meditation are particularly interesting. Another interesting idea which Mr. Martz has advanced is the existence of a middle ground of the creative mind in which the two arts, meditation and poetry, meet to form a poetry of meditation.

In the same year (1954) E. I. Watkin published his *Poets and Mystics*, a work representing the most significant contribution to the study of the mystical and meditative aspects of

Crashaw's lyrics since Miss White's *The Metaphysical Poets.*
Mr. Watkin studies the themes which are most often the
subject of Crashaw's meditations and stresses the characteristic qualities of "pure adoration and contemplation." He
attacks the problem of erotic imagery head on, asserting that
what we encounter here is not a sublimation of the sexual
impulse but rather sexual union seen as the shadow of the
union of the spirit with God; this divine union is the substance, the physical nuptial merely its least inadequate reflection. Even Mr. Watkin, however, calls attention to Crashaw's "half-feminine nature," presumably because of his
fondness for breast and nest imagery. More enlightening,
however, are his observations on the blood, wound, and dart
imagery. These attest love; even the tears at the foot of the
cross are basically happy.

Eleanor M. McCann's unpublished dissertation (Stanford,
1953) *The Influence of Sixteenth and Seventeenth Century
Spanish Mystics and Ascetics on Some Metaphysical Writers*
is the best study available treating the relationship between
the Spanish mystics and the English poets of the Renaissance,
with special emphasis on St. Teresa of Avila and John Donne.
She demonstrates influence where one would least expect it,
attributing to Spanish mysticism not only the addition of
romantic fervor to harsh asceticism, the extreme use of
bodily eating to suggest spiritual nourishment, but especially
the exercise of the spirit of toleration. Also worthy of development is her suggestion that once the mystical writers succeeded in externalizing the spiritual life, the wit and ingenuity of the artist could be turned loose in the arrangement of
these outer symbols. Less felicitous is her contention that
Crashaw is not much concerned with the really deep, internal
aspects of the soul's life. Another significant contribution is
Miss McCann's observation that Spain, not Italy, is the birth-

place of the "violent combination of opposites." She also points out the role medieval scholastic philosophers played in the acceptance of the tradition of erotic imagery and in the general use of vivid metaphor in discussing spiritual matters.

Robert M. Adams, in "Taste and Bad Taste in Metaphysical Poetry" (*Hudson Review*, 1955) quite properly calls attention to changes in taste and attitudes which make Crashaw unpalatable for some modern readers, and he stresses the tension in Crashaw's poetry produced by the uniting of feelings and thoughts between which common sense maintains a degree of antipathy. Many of these clashing opposites, much of the imagery which becomes (to Mr. Adams) a phantasmagoria, seem much less exotic when viewed in a purely symbolic context.

But viewing Crashaw's images as purely symbolic is precisely what most critics will not do. Even Arno Esch, in his *Englische Religiöse Lyrik des 17. Jahrhunderts* (1955) finds nothing better to say about "To the Wounds of Our Crucified Lord" than that this lyric "schwelgt in blut und wunden." For Esch, as for Praz, "The Weeper" is a mere rosary of epigrams and Crashaw's works in general are concocted of a not too pleasant mixture of "femininer Sensibilität und ekstatischer Pathetik." In Chapter V he compares Crashaw's translations of medieval hymns with their original and, naturally, to Crashaw's detriment. Nevertheless, Esch's book performs a significant service in its stress on God's mysterious love for man as Crashaw's "Hauptthema," a point which the author develops admirably.

Perhaps the most brilliant contribution to Crashaw scholarship during the last twenty-three years is Stephen Manning's article "The Meaning of 'The Weeper'" (*ELH*, 1955). This study, so perceptive of the subtlest nuances and yet so sane, so firmly rooted in historical understanding, is a refreshing example of what can be achieved by a judicious blend of the historical approach and the "new criticism." Mr. Manning's detailed analysis of "The Weeper" succeeds as it does precisely because the critic is fully cognizant of the emblematic nature of Crashaw's imagery and is quite familiar with the history of Christian symbolism—indispensable equipment for anyone who hopes to write accurately about religious lyrics of the seventeenth century. Still, some of the particulars of Mr. Manning's interpretation, especially his treatment of the highly ornamental passages, are open to challenge.

Much more open to challenge, however, are some of the statements in Wylie Sypher's fascinating book *Four Stages of Renaissance Style* (1955). What an astute reader is especially likely to challenge is the author's glib drawing of parallels between the arts. Nevertheless, Sypher's distinctions between "mannerism" and "the Baroque" are useful and even valid up to a point if not pushed too far. The book contains excellent material on the role played by the Council of Trent and the Counter-Reformation in the evolution of the Baroque spirit, but like Austin Warren he overemphasizes the importance of this role. Critics need to remind themselves constantly that Crashaw developed his poetic style while an apparently contented Anglican, and that his countrymen did not consider it bizarre.

Another critic of the fifties whose contributions have been substantial is Mary Ellen Rickey. Her two studies of possible sources of (and influences on) Crashaw's lyrics are far saner and more modest in their claims than source studies usually are: "Chapman and Crashaw" (*N & Q*, 1955), "Crashaw and Vaughan" (*N & Q*, 1955). Her major contribution, published in 1961, will be discussed toward the end of this chapter.

In 1956 Mr. George Williams published an intriguing little

article entitled "Crashaw and the Little Gidding Book-binders" (*N & Q*), and Mr. Goldfarb, in "Suppose He Had Been Tabled at Thy Teates" (*Explicator*, 1956) added his force to Miss Tuve's in the attack on William Empson's interpretations of seventeenth-century poetry. Like Miss Tuve, Mr. Goldfarb demonstrates the advantage of Bible reading for the literary critic, but his own interpretation of this controversial passage would have been far sounder had he been more keenly aware of the symbolical possibilities of Crashaw's language; specifically, of the fact that physical nourishment usually symbolizes spiritual nourishment.

One narrow aspect of this symbolical nature of Crashaw's language has been studied by Robert Collmer in "Crashaw's 'Death more misticall and high'" (*JEGP*, 1956). Mr. Collmer's thesis is that Crashaw used the word *death* with a meaning different from the ordinary seventeenth-century denotation. Crashaw most often means, according to Collmer, not death of the soul (*pace* Warren) but that exodus out of self which is generally known as "contemplation," that state in which the soul is stripped not only of desire for corporeal things but also of all images derived from them. What Crashaw scholarship badly needs is a study of Crashaw's religious poetry in *relationship* to the contemplative state briefly described above. Also bolstering the theses upholding the intellectual side of Crashaw is Laura Pettoello's article "A Current Misconception Concerning the Influence of Marino's Poetry on Crashaw's" (*MLR*, 1957), which demonstrates that the influence of Marino has been both misunderstood and over-emphasized: there is far more "brainwork" and elaboration in Crashaw than in Marino.

A short bibliographical study by J. E. Savenson, "Richard Crashaw" (*TLS*, 1957) and an interesting analysis of an old anthology favorite, William Madsen's "A Reading of 'Music's

Duel' " (*Studies in Honor of John Wilcox,* Wayne University, 1958) were followed by the highly significant contribution of Julius Locke—*Images and Image Symbolized in Metaphysical Poetry with Special Reference to Otherworldliness* (University of Florida, 1958). Refreshingly, Mr. Locke finds that nothing is so characteristic of Crashaw's imagery as its "otherworldly" nature. Crashaw's image, typically disembodied from a "this-worldly spatiotemporal context" (the extended object in fixed space), suggests a transcendence of material limitations and determinations and shows a "strong attraction toward the boundlessness of the immaterial." This desire to transcend the limited materiality of the world is typical also of the pictorial art which Mr. Sypher calls Baroque (as distinct from Manneristic). Mr. Locke is the first critic to develop such a thesis in detail. Crashaw's imagery has, for Mr. Locke, a spiritual immediacy; it purposely lacks the immediacy of an empirical organization of sense imagery. Even the blood, Mr. Locke believes, is purely symbolic, not at all physical. The emphasis of this critical study is a needed corrective to those viewpoints (almost cliches by now) in which the Körporlichkeit (corporality) of the Baroque appears as a pandering to the senses.

The decade closes with the publication of Jean Pierre Attal's "Richard Crashaw" (*Critique,* 1959) and Spartaco Gamberini's *Poeti Metafisici e Cavalieri in Inghilterra.* Neither has anything new to say about Crashaw. Mario Praz long ago complained that in Crashaw the spiritual ended by becoming material, and Gamberini has followed suit.

So has Robert Ellrodt. That brilliant perceptiveness which characterizes his treatment of Marvell is sadly lacking when he concludes that Crashaw loses himself in his sensuous images. (*L'Inspiration Personnelle et l'Esprit Du Temps chez Les Poétes Métaphysiques Anglais, Premiere Partie, Tome I,*

John Donne et les Poétes de la Tradition Chretienne, Paris, 1960, p. 378.)

The thesis of Mary Ellen Rickey's *Rhyme and Meaning in Crashaw* (1961) is that the short lyric and long complimentary poem fused their characteristics to produce the sort of verse which one thinks of as typical of Crashaw: the long topical lyric with its repetition of whole words, phrases, and clauses to dramatize the contrasts and ambiguities of which the epigrammatists were so fond. Another of Miss Rickey's contributions is her demonstration of the role which rhyme plays in Crashaw's lyrics; in fact, Crashaw stresses rhyme even more than Marino does, but for *intellectual* purposes.

Also welcome is Lowry Nelson's *Baroque Lyric Poetry,* which discards one of the most common explanations for the Baroque—an attempt to embrace extremes, or the tension generated by the simultaneous presence of sensualism and spirituality. Mr. Lowry suggests new approaches to the Baroque, stressing the rhetorical audience, heightened awareness of time, and the trend toward particularization. These last two are especially interesting, but one can unearth influences far more tangible than the Zeitgeist—items such as devotional manuals and methods of meditation, the Ignatian and the Salesian. Perhaps Mr. Lowry's delving into the history of the conceit is a misplacing of emphasis; the emblem rather than the conceit lies at the heart of those lyrics which he classifies as Baroque.

The importance of considering the two methods of meditation alluded to above is brought to the fore by a recent study, *The School of Donne* (1961) by Alfred Alvarez. No book treating Crashaw is harder to evaluate, for Mr. Alvarez's study is compounded of old errors, a few new ones, and some brilliant insights. The critic sees in Crashaw a clash between ornamental logical ingenuity and an overall impressionism.

And yet impressionistic is precisely what Crashaw is not. He complains that Crashaw forces the idea of sweetness on everything he approves of, without considering the etymology of this important word; he commends Empson's analysis of the alleged sexual overtones in "The Hymn to the Name and Honor of the Admirable Saint Teresa." Perhaps a more intimate acquaintance with devotional manuals of the seventeenth century and with seventeenth-century methods of meditation would lead to a very different evaluation of the religious lyrics. But there are more dangerous statements in the book; this one, for instance: "An image earns its place if it evokes the apt sensation." (p. 96) "OR!" one is tempted to add, "if it evokes the proper concept." But to strike a more positive note—Mr. Alvarez makes an important point in stressing the public, rhetorical nature of Crashaw's lyrics, although he does not relate this characteristic to the advancing tide of neoclassicism.

Frank Warnke's *European Metaphysical Poetry* (Yale, 1961) merely touches upon Crashaw but merits treatment here because it proposes a highly relevant definition of the Baroque. (The first such study to do so was R. Wellek's "The Concept of Baroque in Literary Scholarship," *JA*, 5, pp. 77–108.) Mr. Warnke proposes that we apply the term *Baroque* to the period extending from the late sixteenth century, replacing the term *seventeenth century* or *late Renaissance*. The Baroque would be subdivided into two phases, the earlier *metaphysical* one (Donne, Herbert) and the later *High Baroque* (Crashaw, Fletcher). The latter is seen as a hyperextension of Renaissance literary techniques rather than as a revolt against these.

While Mr. Warnke is quite right in suggesting terminology which makes the proposed distinctions, that which he suggests would perhaps obscure the impact of the rising tide of neoclassicism and the substantial influence of Spenser and the Elizabethan lyricists. And to characterize the High Baroque chiefly as a hyperextension of the Renaissance techniques is to minimize the substantial modification of earlier techniques and the absorption of new influences.

The Latin Epigrams of Richard Crashaw: with Introduction, English Translation, and Notes, a doctoral thesis by Sister Maris Stella (Milhaupt) (Ann Arbor, 1963), translates and relates Crashaw's epigrams to their generic antecedents, examines more fully than does Austin Warren the liturgical and scriptual sources upon which Crashaw drew, and studies the structure and rhetorical devices of the epigrams, finding the characteristic structural device to be the juxtaposition of two incidents so that one is seen within the context of the other.

More recently Allan Pritchard (*TLS,* July 2, 1964) has published an interesting article entitled "Puritan Charges against Crashaw and Beaumont," which does much to explain why Crashaw left Peterhouse before the full tide of Puritan reforms swept over Cambridge, and proves beyond a doubt his high church sympathies.

In the same year George Walton Williams' *Image and Symbol in the Sacred Poetry of Richard Crashaw* developed the study of Crashaw's imagery initiated twenty-four years ago by Austin Warren. Williams deals with Crashaw's symbolic uses of quantity, white, and red, light and dark liquidity, animals, fire and the instruments of love, and the crucifixion and the instruments of hate. The religious lyrics are also considered in relation to Ptolemaic cosmology. The book is rich in apt illustrations and discusses Crashaw's debt not only to St. Teresa but also to Dionysius the Areopagite. Mr. Williams is the first to have done some justice to this second influence.

In progress is a work by a Swedish scholar, Professor

C. Schaar, entitled *Marino and Crashaw: Sospetto d'Herode, A Commentary*. Dr. Schaar's work is a commentary on both the Italian and the English version of the *Sospetto*, and is fundamentally a study of literary associations—that is, evocative allusions to classical poetry, the Bible, the Church Fathers, Dante and Petrarch—and their effect on the two versions of the *Sospetto*. This study tries to show how our appreciation and interpretation of details in the texts changes as we see them, as it were, against different backdrops. Professor Schaar's analysis also includes some new ideas about archetypes and the importance in epic contexts of various key episodes.

Since the twenties Crashaw scholarship has not been of one cloth. At first glance it appears as a bewildering patchwork of views. And yet, without too much straining, one can arrange almost all critics in two camps: those who are cognizant of the purely symbolic and emblematic nature of Crashaw's imagery and who are familiar with the history of Christian thought and devotion; and those who are unable or unwilling to assume the necessary historical orientation. It is hard to resist pointing out that in the forefront of the first group are American scholars. This survey and assessment concludes in a minor key: generally speaking, the body of criticism on Crashaw's poetry forms the least satisfactory part of seventeenth-century literary scholarship.

APPENDIX II

The Imagery in Certain Representative Lyrics

The general student of Crashaw may welcome a close look at certain lyrics, chosen for their representative use of imagery.

There is no better way to get at the heart of Crashaw's poetic method than to compare his adaptations of medieval hymns with the originals. A frequently maligned passage is the beginning of the last stanza of Crashaw's translation of the hymn "Sancta Maria Dolorum":

> O, let me suck the wine
> So long of this chaste vine,
> Till, drunk of the dear wounds, I be
> A lost thing to the world, as it to me!

Our poet describes his adaptation as "A Pathetical descant upon the plainsong of 'Stabat Mater dolorosa.'" The four lines quoted above represent Crashaw's version of stanza seventeen of the "Stabat Mater":

16. Fac ut portem Christi mortem,
    Passionis fac consortem,
    Et plagas recolere.

17. Fac me plagis vulnerari
    Fac me cruce inebriari,
    Et cruore Filii

(Translation)

16. Grant that I may re-live
    The death of Christ,
    Grant that I may be a companion in His suffering,
    And feel His wounds.

17. Grant that I may be wounded with His wounds,
    Intoxicated by His cross,
    And by the blood of the Son.

For the basic conceit (inebriation by the wounds and blood of Christ) Crashaw is indebted to stanza seventeen. In Crashaw's version there is greater complexity of both image and concept. Both have received elaboration, although the emblem, by reason of its terseness, deserves to be classified as a *contracted* one. And it is interesting that in Crashaw's version one is less conscious of gore. The chaste vine (traditional symbol) is Christ, Whose physical destruction (trampling of grapes) produces the wine, symbol of joy. The wine is the wounds of Christ, a source of joy because they open the gates of Paradise. The poet wishes to suck this wine (contemplate the mystery of Christ's ineffable love for mankind) until spiritually inebriated (until he has risen above the purely rational mode of cognition in all-consuming contemplation).

Then will all worldly pleasures and concerns fade into insignificance. These four lines, then, are a terse rendition of the analysis offered above.

One cannot help noting the mixture of figurative and literal elements. The wine is both a symbol (of joy) and, quite literally, the wounds inflicted on Christ during the Crucifixion, which (literally again) have redeemed mankind. This gliding from image to image sometimes, but by no means always, involves the sudden mixing of metaphors, and this mixing occurs most often in those passages where the poet is trying to focus as much thought as possible into a single image. As Mr. George Williams justly points out, this very readiness to mix metaphors points to the conceptual basis of Crashaw's imagery.

Poems on the Crucifixion seem to invite the embellishment of the extended emblem. In "On the Wounds of Our Crucified Lord" it is especially clear how each detail of ornamentation follows not only the contours of the thought which it embodies but enhances the firm, rigid structure of the whole.

> O These wakeful wounds of Thine!
>   Are they mouths? or are they eyes?
> Be they mouths, or be they eyne,
>   Each bleeding part some one supplies.
>
> Lo, a mouth! whose full-bloom'd lips
>   At too dear a rate are roses.
> Lo, a blood-shot eye! that weeps
>   And many a cruel tear discloses.
>
> O thou that on this foot hast laid
>   Many a kiss and many a tear,
> Now thou shalt have all repaid,
>   Whatsoe'er thy charges were.

This foot hath got a mouth and lips,
  To pay the sweet sum of thy kisses;
To pay thy tears, an eye that weeps,
  Instead of tears, such gems as this is.

The difference only this appears,
  Nor can the change offend,
The debt is paid in ruby tears,
  Which thou in pearls did lend.

The first stanza serves the purpose of introducing the controlling imagery of the poem and of startling the reader into devout attention by an unexpected comparison of Christ's wounds to mouths and eyes. The conceit seems to confirm, at first, the charges of Mr. Alvarez; for at this point it is not clear *why* the poet should choose to develop this peculiar image. But one should keep in mind that an important purpose of strange conceits in religious Baroque poetry is to stimulate wonder, to focus attention, to delight (and thus more easily and more effectively teach), and to prevent the stock response.

The second stanza also tends to support such a charge, although the development of the mouth and eye images serves some sort of intellectual purpose. At this point in the poetic meditation, the preciousness of Christ's blood and the intense suffering during the Crucifixion easily suggest themselves. The first two lines (development of mouth image) underscore the first concept; the last two lines (development of eye image), the second. Particularly interesting is the third line of the second stanza, where the poet un-metaphors a popular metaphor: the eyes of the Saviour are literally covered with blood. This fairly common Baroque device, the un-metaphoring of popular and literary metaphors, has received amazingly little attention, though Rosalie Collie has made a good start in her brilliant study of Marvell (*My Echoing Song*).

The third and fourth stanzas reveal the organization and "meaning" of the poem; and, to both this organization and meaning, the mouth and eye images are crucial. Those who have kised the feet of Jesus (subjected themselves to Him in loving humility) and shed tears at the foot of the cross (repented and wept over their sins, especially because of the price which had to be paid to blot them out) shall be fully repaid by Christ's redemptive act of love. Mouth shall repay mouth; eye (tears) shall reward eye (tears). The last stanza contains another ingenious development of image. The sinner's tears are pearls (white), but Christ's are rubies (red). This is not a sharp juxtaposition merely for the sake of epigrammatic point. Embodied herein is the last thought which the poet hopes to leave with the reader: the high price which Christ paid to redeem him. The ruby symbolizes ardent love; but within the metaphoric design of this poem, it also symbolizes suffering, because of its redness, and preciousness because of its status as a gem. Love manifests itself by willingness to suffer. This suffering is precious not only because of the divinity of the Victim, but also because of its supernatural effects. And that the ruby is an exotic and uncommonly beautiful gem also fits the conceptual design of the poem, for the concepts are viewed as extraordinary and ineffably beautiful. In short, all the concepts of the poem converge and mingle in the ruby symbol: conceptual and esthetic responses are in perfect co-articulation.

A substantial meditation on the Crucifixion has been expressed almost entirely by symbolic means. It is not hard to picture a complex emblem with the wounds of Christ appearing in the form of small red mouths and eyes and with worshippers kneeling, one kissing the left foot of Christ, while another permits large white, globular tears to fall on the right foot. The poem is essentially a verse meditation on such an emblem, one which follows the method of meditation developed by St. Francis de Sales. Imagistic development, then, although ingeniously ornamented, follows the exigencies of the meditative thought. Embellishment is the means, not the end.

Occasionally, Crashaw's emblematism becomes full-fledged allegory, for instance in stanzas 7–9 from "On a Prayer Book Sent to Mrs. N.R.":

> But if the noble bridegroom when He comes
> Shall find the wand'ring heart from home,
>   Leaving her chaste abode
>   To gad abroad:
> Amongst the gay mates of the god of flies
>   To take her pleasure, and to play
>   And keep the Devil's holy day:
> To dance in the sunshine of some smiling,
>   But beguiling
>
>   [second stanza]
>
> Spheres of sweet and sugar'd lies,
>   Some slippery pair
>   Of false, perhaps, as fair
> Flattering, but foreswearing eyes.
>
> Doubtless some other heart
>   Will get the start
> Meanwhile, and, stepping in before,
> Will take possession of that sacred store
>   Of hidden sweets, and holy joys,
>   Words which are not heard with ears—

What we have here is a little spiritual story narrated symbolically. With little effort one can imagine its presentation on a medieval stage, with Anima and Christ playing the principal roles. The only thorny section is the ninth stanza, where Crashaw embellishes the *Canticle of Canticles* with the addition of a rival beloved, one who apparently has a good chance of supplanting Anima. But this analysis is a trifle unfair. The addition of the rival beloved, which appears to be a touch of preciosity at first glance, is related to a belief prevalent during the seventeenth century—the necessity of making good use of God's graces, lest they be withheld in the future or given to another, as punishment.

BIBLIOGRAPHY

Adams, Robert M. "Taste and Bad Taste in Metaphysical Poetry: Richard Crashaw and Dylan Thomas." *Hudson Review,* VIII (Spring 1955), 61–77.

Allison, A. F. "Crashaw and St. Francis de Sales." *RES,* XXIV (October 1948), 295–302.

Alvarez, A. *The School of Donne.* London, 1961.

Anderson, James Bruce. "Richard Crashaw, St. Teresa, and St. John of the Cross." *Discourse,* X, iv (Autumn 1967), 421–428.

Appelbe, Jane Lund. "An Inquiry into the Rehabilitation of Certain Seventeenth Century Poets, 1800–1832" (Dissertation, University of Toronto, 1965). *Dissertation Abstracts,* XXVIIA: 177A–1778A (December 1966).

Barker, Francis E. "Crashaw and Andrewes." *TLS,* 21 August 1937, 608.

Beachcroft, T. O. "Crashaw and the Baroque Style." *Criterion,* XXIII (April 1934), 407–425.

Bennett, Joan. *Four Metaphysical Poets.* Cambridge, 1934.

Bernard, Miriam. "More than a Woman." *Catholic World,* XLX (October 1944), 52–53.

Bertonasco, Marc. *The Intellectual Element in the Religious Lyrics of Richard Crashaw.* Dissertation, University of Wisconsin, 1964.

———— "A New Look at Crashaw and the 'Weeper.'" *Texas Studies in Literature and Language,* X, ii (Summer 1968), 177–188.

———— "Crashaw and the Emblem." *English Studies,* XLIX, vi (December 1968), 530–534.

———— Review of Mario Praz' *"Studies in Seventeenth Century Imagery." English Studies,* XLVII, xi (December 1966), 449–451.

Buckley, Vincent. *Poetry and the Sacred.* London, 1968.

Cammell, C. R. "The Divine Poet." *N & ER,* CXXXV (1950), 230–235.

Chalmers (Lord). "Richard Crashaw: Poet and Saint." *In Memor-*

iam Adolphus William Ward, Master of Peterhouse. Cambridge, 1924.

Chambers, Leland. "In Defense of 'The Weeper.'" *Papers on Language and Literature,* III, ii (Spring 1967), 111–121.

Chapman, Gerald Wester, ed. *Literary Criticism in England—1600–1800.* New York, 1966.

Clayborough, Arthur. *The Grotesque in English Literature.* Great Britain, 1965.

Colby, Elbridge. *English Catholic Poets.* Milwaukee, 1936.

Collmer, Robert G. "Crashaw's Death more misticall and high." *Journal of English and Germanic Philology,* LV (July 1956), 373–380.

Confrey, Burton. "A Note on Richard Crashaw." *Modern Language Notes,* XXXVII (April, 1922), 250–251.

Courthope. *History of English Literature.* London, 1905.

"Devotional Poetry: Donne to Wesley" (annoymous article). *TLS,* 24 December, 1930, 814.

Doughty, William L. *Studies in the Religious Poetry of the Seventeenth Century.* London, 1947.

Eliot, T. S. *For Lancelot Andrewes.* London, 1928.

Ellrodt, Robert. *L'Inspiration Personnelle et l'Esprit Du Temps chez les Poétes Métaphysiques Anglais, Premiere Partie, Tome I, John Donne et les Poétes de la Tradition Chretienne.* Paris, 1960.

Elwert, Theodor, W. "Zur Characteristik der Italienischen Barocklyrik." *Romantisches Jahrbuch* (1950), 421–498.

Empson, William. *Seven Types of Ambiguity.* London, 1956.

Enright, D. J. "George Herbert and the Devotional Poets." *From Donne to Marvell* (ed. B. Ford). Baltimore, 1962.

Esch, Arno. *Englische Religiöse Lyrik des 17 Jahrhunderts, Studien zu Donne, Herbert, Crashaw, Vaughan.* Tübingen, 1955.

Falls, Cyril. "The Divine Poet," *The Nineteenth Century,* XCIII (February 1923), 225–232.

Gamberini, Spartaco. *Poeti Metafisici e Cavalieri in Inghilterra.* Florence, 1959.

Geha, Richard, Jr. "Richard Crashaw: (1613?–1650?) The Ego's Soft Fall." *American Imago,* XXIII, ii (Summer 1966), 158–168.

Goldfarb, Russel M. "Crashaw's 'Suppose He Had Been Tabled at thy Teates.'" *Explicator,* XIX. 6, 35.

Grierson, Sir Herbert. *English Literature during the first Half of the Seventeenth Century*. London, 1906.

Hunter, Jim. *The Metaphysical Poets*. London, 1965.

Itrat-Husain. *The Mystical Element in the Metaphysical Poets of the Seventeenth Century*. Edinburgh, 1948.

Javernick, Stephanie. "Crashaw's Hymme auf Santa Teresa." *NS (Die Neueren Sprachan)*, XIV (1965), 449–461.

Jennings, Elizabeth. *Christian Poetry*. New York, 1965.

Lea, Kathleen M. "Conceits." *Modern Language Review*, XX (October 1925), 389–406.

Locke, Julius D. *Images and Image Symbolized in Metaphysical Poetry with Special Reference to Otherworldliness*. Dissertation, University of Florida, 1958.

Madsen, William G., "A Reading of 'Musicks Duell.'" *Studies in Honor of John Wilcox*. Detroit: Wayne University Press, 1958.

McCann, Eleanor M. *The Influence of Sixteenth and Seventeenth Century Spanish Mystics and Ascetics on Some Metaphysical Writers*. Dissertation, Stanford University, 1953.

Manning, Stephen. "The Meaning of 'The Weeper.'" *ELH*, XXII (March 1955), 34–47.

Martin, L. C. "An Unedited Crashaw Manuscript." *TLS*, 18 April 1952, 272.

Martz, Louis L. *The Poetry of Meditation*. New Haven, 1954.

——— *The Poem of the Mind*. New York, 1966.

——— *The Wit of Love*. Notre Dame, 1969.

Megroz, R. L. *Francis Thompson: The Poet of Heaven and Earth*. London, 1927.

Meyer, Robert Holt. "Seventeenth Century Contemplative Poetry: An Imitation of Mystical Experience" (Dissertation, University of California at Davis, 1966). *Dissertation Abstracts*, XXVIIA: 2504A (February 1967).

Miles, Josephine, and Hana C. Selvin. "A Factor Analysis of the Vocabulary of Poetry in the Seventeenth Century." *The Computer and Literary Style: Introductory Essays and Studies* (ed. Jacob Leed). *Kent Studies in English*. Kent, Ohio, 1966.

Milhaupt, Sister Maris Stella. *The Latin Epigrams of Richard Crashaw: with Introduction, English Translation, and Notes*. Dissertation, University of Michigan, 1963.

Miller, David Merlin. "A Study of Modern Criticism and the Metaphysical Poets of the Seventeenth Century" (Dissertation, University of California at Davis, 1966). *Dissertation Abstracts,* XXVIIA: 2505A (February 1967).

Moloney, Michael F. "Richard Crashaw." *Catholic World,* CLXII (October 1945), 43–45.

de Mourgues, Odette. *Metaphysical, Baroque, and Précieux Poetry.* Oxford, 1953.

Neill, Kerby. "Structure and Symbol in Crashaw's 'Hymn in the Nativity.'" *PMLA,* LXIII (March 1948), 101–113.

Nelson, Lowry. *Baroque Lyric Poetry.* New Haven, 1961.

Nethercot, Arthur H. "The Reputation of the 'Metaphysical Poets' during the Age of Pope." *PQ,* IV (1925), 161–179.

Ong, Walter J. "Wit and Mystery: A Revaluation in Medieval Hymnody." *Speculum,* XXV, 310–41.

Osmond, Percy H. *The Mystical Poets of the English Church.* New York, 1919.

Peter, John. "Crashaw and 'The Weeper.'" *Scrutiny,* XIX (October 1953), 258–273.

Pettoello, Laura. "A Current Misconception Concerning the Influence of Marino's Poetry on Crashaw's." *Modern Language Review,* LII (July 1957), 321–328.

"Poet and Saint" (anonymous article), *TLS,* June 1946, 258.

Praz, Mario. "A Source for an Epigram of Crashaw." *TLS,* 21 October 1949, 681.

——— "Drummond and Crashaw," *TLS,* 21 October 1949, 681.

——— *Secentismo e Marinismo in Inghilterra: John Donne, Richard Crashaw.* Florence, 1926.

——— *Studi sul Concettismo.* Milan, 1934.

——— *Studies in Seventeenth Century Imagery.* The Warburg Institute, University of London, 1939–1947.

Pritchard, Allan. "Puritan Charges against Crashaw and Beaumont." *TLS,* July 2, 1964, 578.

Raspa, Anthony. "Crashaw and the Jesuit Poetic." *University of Toronto Quarterly,* XXXVI (October 1966), 37–54.

Rickey, Mary Ellen. "Chapman and Crashaw." *Notes and Queries,* CCI (November, 1956), 472–73.

——— "Crashaw and Vaughan." *Notes and Queries,* CC (June, 1955) 232–33.

——— *Rhyme and Meaning in Richard Crashaw*. Lexington: University of Kentucky Press, 1961.

Scott, W. S. *The Fantasticks: John Donne, George Herbert, Richard Crashaw, Henry Vaughan*, London, 1948.

Seventeenth Century Poetry: The Schools of Donne and Jonson ed. Hugh Kenner). New York, 1964. Anon. rev., *Seventeenth Century News*, XXIII, i & ii (Spring & Summer 1965).

Seymour-Smith, Martin. *Poets Through Their Letters*. New York, 1969.

Sharp, Robert L. *From Donne to Dryden, the Revolt Against Metaphysical Poetry*. Chapel Hill, North Carolina, 1940.

Spender, Constance. "Richard Crashaw, 1613–1648." *Contemporary Review*, CXVI (August 1919), 210–215.

Starkman, Miriam K., ed. *Seventeenth Century English Poetry*. New York, 1967.

Stanwood, P. G. "Crashaw At Rome." *Notes and Queries*, XXII, vii (July 1966), 256–257.

Stewart, Stanley. *The Enclosed Garden: Tradition and Image in Seventeenth Century Poetry*. Madison, Wisconsin, 1966.

Strier, Richard. "Crashaw's Other Voice." *Studies in English Literature*, IX, i (Winter 1969), 135–151.

Sypher, Wylie. *Four Stages of Renaissance Style*. New York, 1955.

Tholen, Wilhelm. "Ein Englischer Dichter und Mystiker der Barockzeit." *Das Neue Ufer* (1927).

Turnell, Martin. "Richard Crashaw after 300 Years," *Nineteenth Century*, CXLVI (August 1949), 100–114.

——— *Studies in Seventeenth Century Poetic*. Madison, Wisconsin, 1950.

Wajda, Edward Joseph. "The Phoenix Legend in Seventeenth Century Literature" (Dissertation, Arizona State University, 1968). *Dissertation Abstracts*, XXIX: 1216A (October 1968).

Wallerstein, Ruth. *Studies in Seventeenth Century Poetic*. Madison, Wisconsin, 1950.

Warnke, Frank. *European Metaphysical Poetry*. New Haven, Connecticut, 1961.

Warren, Austin. "Crashaw and St. Teresa." *TLS*, 25 August 1932, 593.

——— "Crashaw Epigramomata Saca," *JEGP*, XXXIII (April 1932), 233–239.

———— "Crashaw's Paintings in Cambridge," *MLN*, XLVIII
(1933), 233–239.

———— "Crashaw's Reputation in the Nineteenth Century,"
PMLA, LI (September 1936), 769–785.

———— "Crashaw's Residence at Peterhouse." *TLS*, 3 November
1932, 815.

———— "The Reputation of Crashaw in the Seventeenth and
Eighteenth Centuries." *SP*, XXXI (July 1934), 385–407.

———— *Richard Crashaw: A Study in Baroque Sensibility.* Ann
Arbor, Michigan, 1939, 1957.

Watkin, E. I. *Poets and Mystics.* London, 1954.

White, Helen C. *English Devotional Literature: Prose 1600–1640.
University of Wisconsin Studies in Language and Literature, No.
19,* Madison, 1931.

———— *The Metaphysical Poets: A Study in Religious Experience.*
New York, 1936, 1956.

Willey, Basil. "Richard Crashaw" (Memorial Lecture Delivered at
Peterhouse). Cambridge, England, 11 July 1949.

Williams, George. *Image and Symbol in the Sacred Poetry of Richard Crashaw.* Columbia: University of South Carolina Press,
1963.

Williams, George W. "Richard Crashaw and the Little Gidding
Bookbinders." *Notes and Queries*, XII (1965), 9–10.

Williamson, George. *The Donne Tradition: A Study in English
Poetry from Donne to the Death of Cowley.* Cambridge: Har-
vard University Press, 1930.

Williamson, George. *Six Metaphysical Poets: A Reader's Guide.*
New York, 1967.

Winters, Yvor. *Forms of Discovery.* Chicago, 1967.

Woodhouse, A.S.P. *The Poet and His Faith.* Chicago, 1965.

EDITIONS

The Complete Works of Richard Crashaw. ed. Alexander Grosart.
2 vols. London, 1873.

The Poems of Richard Crashaw. ed. V. R. Tutin, with introd. by
Canon Beeching. London, 1905.

The Poems English Latin and Greek of Richard Crashaw. ed. L. C.
Martin. Oxford, 1927. 2nd ed., rev., 1957.

INDEX